ELIJAH

YESTERDAY, TODAY, AND TOMORROW

ELIJAH

YESTERDAY, TODAY, AND TOMORROW

BYRON R. MERRILL

Bookcraft
Salt Lake City, Utah

Library of Congress Catalog Card Number: 97-73197
ISBN 1-57008-331-2

First Printing, 1997

Printed in the United States of America

Dedicated to the seven most important women in my life, all linked to me by the power Elijah restored:

The legacy of the past—Carma, Elizabeth, and Cynthia, my mother and grandmothers.

The promise of the future—Aimee, Rachel, and Brittany, my precious daughters.

The vision of eternity—my sweetheart, Tricia.

CONTENTS

Appendixes

PREFACE

ELIJAH IS ONE OF THE MOST ENIGMATIC figures of the Old Testament. He appears suddenly, with no prior reader preparation or background information. His first words are an oath and a curse. He is fed by ravens in the wilderness, denounces the acts of the monarchy, calls a fiery blast from heaven atop Mount Carmel, and then retreats to the wilderness to commune with the Lord. He exits in a blaze of glory, transported by a chariot and horses of fire, causing his departure to be even more dramatic and sudden than was his arrival. Then, without as much as a passing reference to Elijah for hundreds of years, the last recorded words in the Old Testament foretell his future return to prepare the world for the coming of the "great and dreadful day of the Lord" (Malachi 4:5–6).

Who was this man? What do we know of him? How was his ministry a type of the Lord's coming? What does Malachi's prophecy of his return foreshadow? How was the prophecy fulfilled or, better yet, how is it being fulfilled? What does all of this mean to each of us, and why is it so critically important? In his book *The Holy Temple*, Elder Boyd K. Packer stated, "Elijah and his ministry are worthy of a book."[1] Written in response to that suggestion, this book is but a beginning in the valuable quest to explore the history and significance of the mission of the prophet and to understand the meaning of "the spirit of Elijah."

It would not be an exaggeration to say that the brief references to Elijah in the King James Version of the Holy Bible—seven short chapters in the books of 1 and 2 Kings, a mention in 2 Chronicles, the two verses at the end of the book of Malachi, and a few references in the New Testament—have generated thousands of traditions and tens of thousands of pages of commentary. In preparation for this book I have checked so many sources, studied so many maps and lexicons, and read so many books, articles, and monographs that I have lost count of their number. But after all the searching, reading, and note taking, there is something wonderfully refreshing about prayerfully seeking the influence of the Spirit and then simply reading and pondering afresh the words of the biblical text that recount the history of Elijah. Thus, in the midst of this search, I have earnestly sought the illumination of the Spirit to enlighten me about what really happened and what it means.

The completion of this work owes a great deal to the encouragement and assistance of others. The inspiration for studying this topic comes from the deep love I have for my eternal companion, Tricia. Reflecting on the covenants we have made has aroused an intense interest about the significance of the prophet Elijah's involvement with the priesthood keys that make those covenants eternally binding. Together my sweetheart and I have spent considerable time searching for our ancestors and performing ordinances for them in the temples of the Lord. The "spirit of Elijah" has been poured out upon us in rich abundance as we have concentrated on this labor of love. Blessings have come to us in all aspects of our lives, often at unexpected moments and from unanticipated directions. The more we have enjoyed of that special spirit, the greater my desire has become to understand it more fully. This book is the result of a quest to answer some of the questions I have asked about this topic over the years.

My arrival at Brigham Young University in 1989 afforded me added opportunity to seriously pursue the study of Elijah's life and mission. Many have assisted me in that study. Brant Bishop and Jared Smartt began the research. Mark Sheffield, Gary Ellis, Bryce Earl, and Ryan Moffat continued it. I am deeply indebted to James Howard for sorting through all the traditions and organizing them in such a way that I could present a brief sampling of them in the appendixes. Patrick Thurston rendered the valuable service of closely reviewing the manuscript and making textual suggestions. I am especially grateful for my friends and colleagues Robert L. Millet and Robert J. Matthews, who have given me continual en-couragement for this undertaking and have provided significant insights into the topic.

To all who have given insights, added clarification for my thoughts, or participated in any manner in bringing this work to fruition, I extend my sincere appreciation. Yet, in the end, this book is a personal expression of my understanding of the life and mission of Elijah. It is not an official statement of either Brigham Young University or The Church of Jesus Christ of Latter-day Saints.

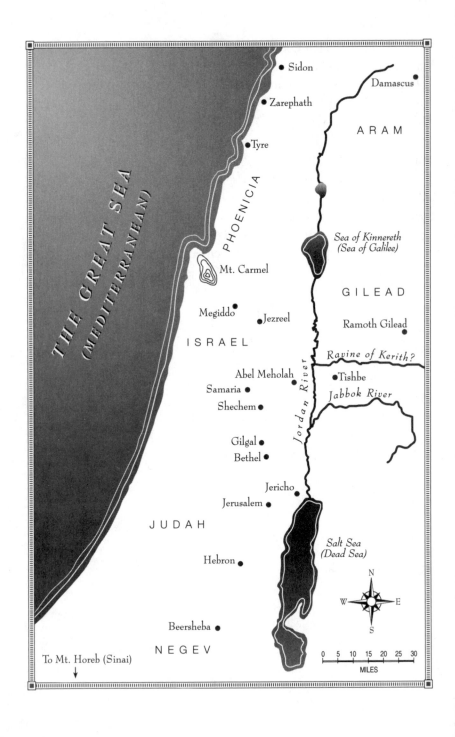

Chapter One

THE
SETTING

THE ANCIENT KINGDOM OF ISRAEL HAD enjoyed an era of great territorial expansion and increased international power under the leadership of its king, David, the son of Jesse, of the tribe of Judah, who ruled from about 1010 to 970 B.C.[1] But as the narrative about Elijah begins, those days were long since past. Few people still lived who had firsthand knowledge of the glories of the reign of King Solomon, who had assumed the throne at the death of his father, King David. A greater number remained who had lived in the days of Solomon's son and successor, Rehoboam. Some of them remembered that Rehoboam had decided to raise taxes on the already burdened tribes of Israel and that, in response, the leaders of the people comprising the northern ten tribes had rejected Rehoboam as their king. Those ten tribes chose instead to follow the leadership of Jeroboam, of the tribe of Ephraim, and seceded from the union previously known as the "United Kingdom." The new confederacy formed by these ten tribes maintained the national name of Israel, while the remaining southern tribes who followed Rehoboam adopted the name of Judah for their kingdom.

Jeroboam, newly appointed as king by the northern tribes, worried that his confederation would crumble if the people continued their worship of Jehovah, the God of Israel. To do so would require them to offer sacrifices according to the law of Moses at the great temple in Jerusalem, which was then under the control of his enemy Judah. He therefore instituted a perverted form of Jehovah worship at Dan and Bethel, cities at the northern and southern extremities of his kingdom. At those sites he set up golden calves, which he commanded his people to worship. In reviewing Jeroboam's life, the Old Testament continually refers to him with the epithet "he made Israel to sin" (1 Kings 15:26).

Let it be noted here that there are many theories about the authorship of the Old Testament books of 1 and 2 Kings, but all are conjectural.[2] 1 Kings 19:3 provides a clue by referring to the city of Beersheba as one "which belongeth to Judah," perhaps suggesting that the author of that portion of the text was from the northern kingdom of Israel. It seems clear that whoever—singular or plural—wrote these books was primarily concerned with recording the children of Israel's maintenance of their peculiar covenant relationship with Jehovah. This covenant was originally made with their ancestor Abraham (see Genesis 17, Abraham 2–3), the Lord promising him and his descendants certain choice blessings if they would faithfully be His ministers and carry His message and power to all peoples of the earth. It was from such a perspective that the author(s) of the books of Kings made strong judgmental statements like those recorded about Jeroboam.

Roughly thirty years and several ruling houses after Jeroboam's death, Omri, the captain of the army of Israel, became king. There followed several years of civil war in which Omri contended for the throne with Tibni, another leader of the people. Ultimately, Omri and his followers prevailed. He was the fifth king of Israel to follow Jeroboam. Like his predecessors, who were without exception labeled as wicked by the author of 1 Kings,[3] Omri followed and undoubtedly promoted the perverted Jehovah worship instigated by Jeroboam at Dan and Bethel.

Omri reigned only twelve years. Midway through his reign he purchased a virgin hill and began building his new capital city, which he called Samaria. Ahab, Omri's son and successor, continued and greatly expanded Samaria's construction. Additionally, he conducted major building projects in prominent fortress cities such as Megiddo and Hazor. Early in the 20th century A.D., archaeologists excavated the site of ancient Samaria, uncovering the magnificent palace of Omri, which Ahab enlarged, with its abundance of ivory objects in confirmation of the scriptural account in 1 Kings 22:39 referring to "the ivory house which he made, and all the cities that he built."[4] This era of growth and expansion displayed a certain sense of grandeur that permitted it to be compared with the reign of Solomon, allowing the northern kingdom and Samaria to be a true rival of Judah and its capital, Jerusalem. Omri thus established a legacy sufficiently significant that when Assyria conquered Israel more than a century later, the conquerors referred to their victory as being over the "house of Omri,"[5] even though the dynasty he founded had long since expired.

The era of Omri and Ahab was one of commercial expansion. It appears to have been a time of dramatic increase in business activity. Syrian "streets"—probably business districts controlled by Syrian merchants—were established in Samaria under Omri, and Israelite "streets" in Damascus, the capital of Syria, under Ahab (see 1 Kings 20:34). The result of all this was a great disparity between the rich and powerful upper class and the poor, defenseless lower class. Such social inequality would bring the condemnation of later prophets. Interestingly, the author of 1 Kings says little about the economic achievements of the era. His relative silence parallels the prophet Mormon's glossing over all the temporal accomplishments of King Noah in the book of Mosiah. Both authors view history through lenses focused on the spiritual well-being of people, not the economic climate.

Geographically and politically, the kingdom of Israel was surrounded by opponents: Judah to the south, Phoenicia to the northwest, and Syria to the northeast. 1 Kings 20:34 makes brief scriptural reference to the fact that Syria had conquered and taken certain cities from Israel in the days of Omri. Following the period of internal civil strife during which his reign began, Omri sought both to unify his kingdom internally and to secure peace externally through political alliances with neighboring rulers. The loss of territory to the king of Syria likely prompted Omri to turn to the Phoenicians for alliances, probably resulting in the arranged marriage between Omri's son Ahab and Jezebel, "the daughter of Ethbaal king of the Zidonians" (1 Kings 16:31).

The mention of Ethbaal brings us to his city, Tyre. Tyre (the modern Sur) lies about 25 miles south of Sidon—both cities being on the Mediterranean coast of modern Lebanon—and about 28 miles north of the coastal city of Akko in modern Israel. Tyre was, at that time, an island fortress (see Ezekiel 27:32). Centuries later, during the time of Alexander the Great, the city was connected to the mainland by a dike that has broadened over the centuries and now forms a peninsula.[6] During Solomon's golden age, he made alliance with Hiram, king of Tyre, who provided materials for building the great temple in Jerusalem (see 1 Kings 5). It appears as though during the following decades the kings of Tyre consolidated their control over all the southern coast of Phoenicia, making them the kings of the Sidonians, or Phoenicians.

Prior to becoming king, Ethbaal had been a priest of the goddess Astarte. It appears that he usurped the throne following the murder of his brother.[7] He began to rule at the age of 36 and reigned for about 32 years.[8] He undoubtedly watched with concern the unrest and rapid succession of kings in the neighboring land of Israel. The desire for political stability likely motivated him and Omri to look favorably upon the union of their children Jezebel and Ahab. The marital union peacefully allied the two kingdoms in approximately 878–872 B.C.[9]

This marriage was a turning point in Israel's history. Although Omri had presided over the decline of Israel's spiritual health to new depths (see 1 Kings 16:25), all that he did was only a prelude to the huge leap into the dark abyss that would be made by his son Ahab. Scripture records that "as if it had been a light thing" (1 Kings 16:31), or, to paraphrase, as if it had been insufficiently evil for Ahab to follow in the sins of Jeroboam, Ahab went a step farther by marrying an idolatress and then embracing the worship of her idol god, Baal. That is, Ahab not only married Jezebel but also married her god.

The very name "Jezebel" means essentially "Baal is prince." In general terms, Baal was the god of nature who, with his consort Asherah—also known as Astarte or Ashteroth (sometimes translated as "the grove(s)" in the Old Testament)—presided over the pantheon of gods worshiped in much of the territory surrounding the kingdom of Israel. Epitomizing this fertility cult, Baal has sometimes been called the producing principle in nature and Asherah the receptive principle in nature.[10]

Decades earlier, Jeroboam had set up altars in Dan and Bethel that were illegal under the law of Moses. Ahab now took the next giant, downward step by building a temple to Baal in Samaria wherein he erected an altar to this pagan deity. It was thus that idolatry, the archenemy of Israel's covenant with the true God, had not just crept in but been invited in as a welcomed guest. It was this act that resulted in the scriptural appraisal: "Ahab did more to provoke the Lord God of Israel to anger than all the kings of Israel that were before him" (1 Kings 16:33).

Some have viewed Ahab as a weak king for allowing his foreign-born queen to superimpose her religion over him and his people. While it seems clear that a Phoenician mentality penetrated all Israelite society under Jezebel's influence, it is hard to view Ahab as a weakling. He reigned over a prosperous and influential nation for 22 years, established a renown for his great building program, conquered the Syrian army under its king Ben-hadad (see 1 Kings 20:21), and then set up commercial enterprises in Damascus. He commanded an army of 2,000 chariots and 10,000 foot soldiers in a battle with Shalmaneser III of Assyria.[11] It seems unlikely that such a man would have let Baal worship slip in the back door. He likely wanted to strengthen his hand in dealing with his neighboring kingdoms, both friend and foe. At that time Phoenicia, of which Tyre and Sidon formed a part, enjoyed great prosperity, sending commercial expeditions to distant ports and establishing colonies throughout the area. Jezebel came from the very family that in succeeding generations would establish the great ancient city of Carthage.

Ahab was thus not a weakling but was very clever. He seems to have felt that embracing the obviously successful Baal was progressive. But as part of his cunning, Ahab dared not totally forsake

Jehovah. His people still worshiped at Jehovah's altars in Dan and Bethel, even though their worship had degenerated into a form of paganism. And he still had to coexist with neighboring Judah, where the law of Moses was followed and temple worship contin-ued. Politically, then, if nothing more, Ahab maintained his affili-ation with the God of Israel. He proceeded to offer overtures of peace to Judah, resulting in the first era of agreement between the two powers since the days of Solomon. The kings of the two coun-tries joined forces to fight their common enemies, Syria and Moab (see 1 Kings 22, 2 Kings 3). Later, Israel and Judah even entered into political alliance through marriage. Athaliah, daughter of Ahab and Jezebel, married Jehoram, the son of Jehoshaphat of Judah (see 2 Kings 8:16–18).

Therefore, without abandoning Jehovah, Ahab nonetheless adopted Baal. While Jehovah provided the old, sure formula for maintaining control at home and political contacts with Judah, Baal seemed to be on the upswing and would cement Ahab's rela-tions with his other neighbors. Ahab's actions exposed his ecu-menical thoughts: "Why not invite Baal in to join Jehovah and have the best of both worlds?"

In the midst of such momentous changes the ancient city of Jericho was rebuilt (see 1 Kings 16:34). Its reconstruction raises several unanswered questions. Was it rebuilt as a fortress city on Israel's southern border to protect against advances by Judah or Moab? Was the builder, Hiel, a supervisor of construction under Ahab's direction or a freelancer at whose efforts Ahab only winked? Whatever the specific circumstances, it is clear that the curse placed by Joshua centuries earlier on the rebuilding of Jericho (see Joshua 6:26) was ignored and, thus, unwittingly activated. The king of Israel challenged or at least ignored this ancient curse at the same moment when a curse of much greater proportions descended upon his whole people because of the idolatry he initiated.

It appears that somehow the events surrounding Hiel's rebuild-ing of Jericho brought Ahab together with Elijah, the subject of this volume. Whatever countermeasures to Israel's growing idola-try the Lord may have taken up to that point in time, whatever priests or prophets had been charged with seeking to stop the spiritual slide of covenant Israel, now that wickedness had brazenly unveiled itself in the attitudes and practices of Ahab and Jezebel the Lord prepared a counteroffensive by unleashing his heavy artillery in the person of Elijah the Tishbite, who was, as one 17th-century cleric labeled him, "the eminentist prophet reserved for the corruptest age."[12]

Chapter Two

THE CONFRONTATION
AND THE BROOK

SPEAKING OF THOSE ERAS OF HISTORY when general wickedness would prevail, Isaiah prophesied, "When the enemy shall come in like a flood, the Spirit of the Lord shall lift up a standard against him" (Isaiah 59:19). Such a crisis existed in the days of Ahab and Jezebel. The flood of wickedness was about to devour all good before it, sweeping it into a dark sea of oblivion. A standard for righteousness needed to be erected; a power to stop the consuming flood must arise. To raise that standard of hope, Jehovah, the God of Israel, sent a prophet, Elijah the Tishbite, a man who spoke with and for the Almighty. Such individuals often appear to the carnal world as outsiders, as "strangers and pilgrims" (1 Peter 2:11). Elijah certainly fit that description. He appears abruptly, without introduction, in 1 Kings 17:1. His first words invoked the power of Israel's God to curse the land: "As the Lord God of Israel liveth, before whom I stand, there shall not be dew nor rain these years, but according to my word" (1 Kings 17:1). Who was this Elijah? Where did he come from? How old was he? What of his training and occupation and previous prophetic experience? Had he met the king before or was this their first encounter? So many questions without answers.

This mysterious figure appears so suddenly in the text as to catch the reader off guard. We are told only that he was Elijah the Tishbite, "of the inhabitants of Gilead" (1 Kings 17:1). What do the various aspects of this brief summary tell us? The name "Elijah" means "Jehovah is God," "Jehovah is my God," or "my God is Jehovah." This may have been his birth name, or perhaps it was the name attributed to him in adulthood due to the nature of his prophetic mission.

Gilead was that portion of ancient Israel east of the Jordan River. It is an area of rugged hills, dry forests, and open spaces, attributes that could be seen to fit Elijah's character as portrayed in the Old Testament. The prophet's title "the Tishbite" has given rise to much conjecture. One commentator has suggested that the title is so close to the Hebrew word for *conversion* that Elijah might have been a Gentile convert.[1] Others assume the phrase is a reference to his being a sojourner and thus wonder if he may have been part of a group of nomads, perhaps a Kenite or Rechabite.[2] Some have even suggested that he may have been an angel, explaining both why we know nothing of his parentage or early life and his being taken to heaven miraculously instead of dying.[3] Another possibility is that the phrase means "the reformer, the changer, the man sent of God Jehovah to cause reform."[4]

Most biblical scholars have looked for a location named Tisbi or Tisbeh as his original home. The traditional site since Byzantine times was a ruin named el-Ishtib—pronounced today Listib—eight miles north of the Jabbok River in the modern nation of Jordan. It is located one mile from a mount and shrine called Mar Elyas, "the Mount of Elijah." If accurate, this designation would place Elijah's home in the ancient area labeled Gilead, east of the Jordan River. Another possibility is a town named Tishbi in the territory of the tribe of Naphtali, the area now called Galilee, known from a story in the apocryphal book of Tobit (1:2, Septuagint). Perhaps he originally came from that town but was living in the area of Gilead at the time of his appearance to Ahab. Yet most modern commentators follow the wording of the early Greek Old Testament, the Septuagint, in placing Elijah's original home in Gilead.[5] As this brief summary shows, there is no consensus on Elijah's birthplace.

When Elijah makes his initial appearance in the Bible, the text portrays him less as the bearer of the message of a coming famine than as its very orchestrator. His first recorded words are "As the Lord God of Israel liveth, before whom I stand . . ." Notice how much he communicated in that brief phrase. He reminded the king that Israel had a special covenant relationship with its God, who was, the prophet attested, still very much alive. Then the prophet made a solemn oath, swearing by the life of Israel's God, that he, Elijah, also had a special relationship with God that gave him authority to speak in God's behalf. As Elijah could swear by no greater Being, either he truly possessed the authority he claimed or he blasphemed. Having stated his authority as the Lord's servant, Elijah then declared, "There shall not be dew nor rain these years, but according to my word."

We have no explanation of what generated this remarkable declaration. Something notable must have preceded it. Also, there is no mention of a response by Ahab. Was he overwhelmed at the power and spirit of the communication? Did the king's previous knowledge of Elijah's power therefore strike him with fear? Or were the two of them strangers? Did Ahab think him a crank or a nut or worse?

It is interesting that the books of ancient Jewish tradition known as the Jerusalem and Babylonian Talmuds relate an apocryphal tale about the meeting of Ahab and Elijah. The story says that both men met at the house of Hiel the Bethelite to console him on the loss of his sons occasioned by the rebuilding of Jericho. In the course of their visit, Ahab reportedly commented to Elijah that it seemed strange that the ancient curse pronounced by Joshua should have been fulfilled by the death of Hiel's sons. The king reasoned that Joshua occupied a secondary position in comparison to the great Moses, and yet Moses' curse on Israel stood unfulfilled. Ahab reminded Elijah that Moses had prophesied that if Israel should ever turn to the worship of other gods, the Lord would withhold the rain in its season (see Deuteronomy 28: 23–24).

But, continued Ahab derisively, even though everyone in Israel worshiped other gods, Moses' curse had still not come about. It was then, according to rabbinic tradition, that Elijah swore with an oath that the promised curse would now begin.[6] We are left to wonder if there is any historical substance to such a tale. A single verse of scripture is all we have.

What about the predicted drought and resulting famine? The rains in Israel usually come from late fall to spring. For the balance of the year, morning dew provides the primary source of moisture. Would the curse pronounced by Elijah allow no moisture at all? For how long? Would not the land wilt and die? Could such a dearth of life-giving moisture be justified as an act of God or of his servant? As terrible as such a curse may be, there are worse things. The physical suffering and calamity occasioned by drought are not nearly so dreadful as moral delinquency and spiritual apostasy. One makes mortality miserable; the other threatens eternity.

To understand Elijah's pronouncement, it is instructive to re- view an analogous situation recorded in the book of Helaman in the Book of Mormon. Nephi, the son of Helaman, had powerfully preached repentance to his people to encourage them to turn from their pride and wickedness. He was rebuffed almost at every turn, however, and even falsely accused of murder. "Being much cast down," he was pondering over the situation of his people when the voice of the Lord came to him, saying: "Blessed art thou, Nephi, for those things which thou hast done. . . . Behold, I will bless thee forever; and I will make thee mighty in word and in deed, in faith and in works; yea, even that all things shall be done unto thee ac- cording to thy word, for thou shalt not ask that which is contrary to my will." (Helaman 10:3–5.) The Lord then bestowed upon Nephi the power to seal and to loose on earth and in heaven (see v. 7). We commonly call this the "sealing power."

Nephi returned to his preaching with such power that some were angered at his words and began to fight among themselves. Before long, warfare broke out. As the people approached certain destruction, Nephi prayed that there might "be a famine in the land, to stir them up in remembrance of the Lord their God, and perhaps they will repent and turn unto thee" (Helaman 11:4). The heavens were sealed at his command and the famine began. Some have wondered why it is better for people to be dying from famine than from war. In warfare, there is always an enemy, someone else to blame, which causes feelings of anger and revenge. But whom can you blame for a famine? There is something about the ebbing of physical strength and energy resulting from lack of food that seems to remove our thoughts from the mundane aspects of everyday life. We tend to become more sober and our thoughts often turn heavenward. In essence, famine may be the last chance to help us understand what it means to fast. For Nephi's people, it worked. They repented and the drought ceased in accordance with Nephi's plea to the Lord.

Would it stretch the limits of reason to see Elijah in a posture similar to Nephi's? Could we not imagine the Lord bestowing upon him the sealing power with words like those spoken to Nephi? Was not the famine in Elijah's day also caused to encourage repentance of a wayward people? Is it not also possible that Nephi announced the coming dearth to the leader of the Nephites in terms as strong as those addressed by Elijah to Ahab? The repentant Nephites pleaded with their leaders to request that Nephi ask the Lord to end the famine, indicating they knew who had been instrumental in bringing it about (see Helaman 11:8). Maybe Elijah was directed by the Lord to go into the desert not just to avoid destruction from the king's wrath but also that he might be removed from the entreaties of the people to end the famine before the Lord's timetable for its full effect had been met.

In 1 Kings 17, first verse, Elijah is speaking in behalf of the Lord. In the verses immediately following, the Lord is speaking to Elijah, instructing him to leave Jericho, flee eastward, and hide by the brook Cherith. The phrase "before Jordan" in verse 3 means "east of Jordan," the word *before* being used in much the same way in Genesis 23:17,19, and 25:18. Thus, Elijah turned eastward, crossed the river Jordan, and probably stayed in one of the many small ravines that carry tributary streams into the Jordan. Reading this chapter, one gains the impression that the Lord is leading Elijah one step at a time, giving him line upon line. We do not know whether Elijah had any idea he would pronounce a curse upon the earth before the inspired words came from his mouth. Nor do we sense that he knew what he was to do after that utterance. He seems to have been acting on faith, as next shown in verse 5: "So he went and did according unto the word of the Lord: for he went and dwelt by the brook Cherith, that is before Jordan." The Lord told him to go and "so he went." A more simple example of faithful obedience would be hard to find.

Note that the information recorded in the Old Testament about Elijah shows him to be both the natural prophetic successor to the great Moses and the forerunner of Christ. Many of the events in Elijah's history are reminiscent of those experienced by Moses. Likewise, much that Elijah did foreshadowed the acts of the Savior. The prophets serve as types of Christ, and such a type is nowhere seen more clearly or in fewer verses than in the seven chapters of 1 and 2 Kings that speak of Elijah. With the extraordinary brevity of information about Elijah, it seems certain that those few items preserved for us in the text are intended to draw our minds back to parallels with Moses and our hearts forward to visions of Christ. The introductory verses about Elijah reflect such types, first in his declaring his commission from God in speaking the Lord's words and second in his departing into the desert. Elijah went into the wilderness for solitude and preparation as did Moses, the desert being a place of temporal refuge and spiritual rejuvenation. Similarly the Savior often sought a solitary place to ponder and pray (see JST, Matthew 4:1; JST, Mark 6:33).

Elijah's experience is one example of many scriptural accounts of divine deliverance. The Lord inspires the righteous to flee before suffering descends on those who remain: Noah boards the ark; Abraham leaves Ur and Haran; Lot is led out of Sodom; Jacob flees across the Jordan to escape from his brother Esau; Lehi leaves Jerusalem before its destruction; Nephi and his followers are spared the wrath of Laman and Lemuel by fleeing; Mosiah abandons the land of Nephi to discover the people of Zarahemla; Joseph and Mary take the infant Jesus to escape Herod's edict; and so on. Elijah's flight into the wilderness adds to and perpetuates this theme of deliverance.

Returning to the account of Elijah, we read that the Lord indicated he would provide for him by commanding ravens to feed him. The ravens brought "bread and flesh" morning and evening (1 Kings 17:6), reminiscent of the bread (manna) and flesh (quail) miraculously provided to the children of Israel as they wandered in the desert under Moses' leadership centuries earlier (see Numbers 11). Some commentators feel that the word *ravens* should be read "merchants"[7] or "Arabs,"[8] depending on the way they view the Hebrew text. Most, though, concur that the word really is ravens. It does not seem likely that the Lord would send Elijah to a desolate area to hide and then send people twice a day to feed him.

Note that Elijah faithfully followed the Lord's bidding in prophesying to Ahab the withholding of rain and dew. He then obediently found his way to the brook Cherith. Even though he was on the Lord's errand, he was not rewarded with delicacies and opulence, but only with the fulfillment of his basic needs. Even the brook, Elijah's only source of water, was destined to dry up "after a while" (1 Kings 17:7). Within a short period, the drought had tightened its grip on the surrounding country and even the lowland streams had ceased to flow. The Lord's promise that blessings will follow obedience does not necessarily include a pledge of luxury and ease. Remember that he said, "It must needs be done in mine own way" (D&C 104:16). Often, when our obedience induces him to open "the windows of heaven" (Malachi 3:10), nothing more emerges from the clouds than a raven carrying food. But, thank the Lord for ravens!

One conclusion we can draw from these events is that, while we know neither the exact location nor physical condition of either Elijah's original home or the brook where he stayed during the famine, he was definitely living in a spiritual wasteland. When Elijah made his first appearance as recorded in 1 Kings 17:1, a famine already existed in the land—a famine of "hearing the words of the Lord" (Amos 8:11). Elijah's actions simply implemented on a temporal scale the spiritual dearth that already prevailed. While the Lord did not provide a life of comfort for Elijah at Cherith, he did preserve his life. As the brook turned to dust, Elijah was once again reminded of his total dependence upon the Lord. And assuredly, the Lord would continue to provide for him, even if it needed to be at the hands of a starving widow.

Chapter Three

THE MIRACLES
AT ZAREPHATH

AFTER HIS SOJOURN OF PERHAPS SEVERAL months at the brook Cherith, Elijah was commanded, "Arise, get thee to Zarephath, which belongeth to Zidon, and dwell there: behold, I have commanded a widow woman there to sustain thee" (1 Kings 17:9). Zarephath? A city of Sidon? Jezebel's own country? Had not the wicked practices of Jezebel and her husband prompted the drought that then choked the land? Was Elijah to be succored and nourished in Jezebel's father's own kingdom? What must have been Elijah's thoughts at this unusual pronouncement? The scriptures record only this: "So he arose and went to Zarephath" (1 Kings 17:10). Again, we see Elijah's remarkable obedience. He did not ask why; he simply "arose and went."

When the Lord calls us to some act of service or unexpected responsibility, do we find excuses because of supposed incapacity or inconvenience? Do we pull out our planners to see if our busy schedules will permit obedience and time for service? Or do we simply "arise and go" as did Elijah? His example is the practical demonstration of the commitment of Nephi, the son of Lehi, another whose life epitomized obedience. As a youth, he volunteered for a dangerous mission with these words: "I will go and do the things which the Lord hath commanded, for I know that the Lord giveth no commandments unto the children of men, save he shall prepare a way for them that they may accomplish the thing which he commandeth them" (1 Nephi 3:7). What a great example of faith and trust, both of which underlie willing obedience! This same Nephi's last recorded words summarize his life: "For thus hath the Lord commanded me, and I must obey. Amen." (2 Nephi 33:15.) It is just such a lifetime of obedience that is encapsulated in the phrase that Elijah "arose and went" to Zarephath.

Zarephath was a city about seven miles south of Sidon on the road to Tyre. In the New Testament, the city is called Sarepta (see Luke 4:26). Anciently, Jacob's blessings on his sons indicated Zebulon's inheritance would extend along the seacoast to Sidon (see Genesis 49:13), including the area of this city. But when Joshua divided the promised land among the tribes of Israel, all this area, including the site of Zarephath—called the Akko plain— fell to the lot of Asher (see Joshua 19:26). This was in accord with Moses' blessings on the tribes recorded in Deuteronomy, where the tribe of Asher was promised, "Let him dip his foot in oil" (33:24), a reference to the fertility of the area and to its principal product, olive oil. But King Solomon later gave this region to King Hiram of Tyre, where its control remained until Elijah's day (see 1 Kings 9:11). The name Zarephath means "refining," coming from a root that signifies a crucible or place where metals are melted. Here, in a symbolic crucible trying his patience and faith, Elijah would be further refined.

Elijah wandered through or around Israel, likely avoiding most populated areas, on his journey from the Jordan River to Zarephath near the seacoast. Perhaps he wondered at the Lord's words that He would sustain Elijah at the hands of a widow woman. But had not Jehovah used ravens as emissaries to feed Elijah recently? Just as ravens were at the low end of the animal kingdom, being considered ritually unclean by the law of Moses (see Leviticus 11:13–15), so a poor widow would have been on the lowest rung of the social ladder. But the Lord said he had commanded her to care for Elijah, so the prophet proceeded on faith.

We know little of this widow, not even her name. She had a single son who must have been fairly young, since the text regularly refers to him as a child and since both Elijah and the widow carried the boy (see 1 Kings 17:19). A widow without children probably received more care in society than one who had them, for it was assumed that children, especially male children, would have the natural obligation to care for their mothers. Having a son meant that the widow's deceased husband had someone to carry on his name and assume his responsibilities. But if her son was young, he would not yet be in a position to provide for her. Therefore, she was probably left without help from any direction.

Had this widow always been poor, or was she reduced to poverty because of the death of her husband? Had her husband died recently as a result of the famine, or long ago, the current dearth simply compounding the depths of her meager existence? The fact that she had a "loft" (1 Kings 17:19) where Elijah could stay means that she had an upper room for guests, a common situation in Near Eastern residences even today. The loft may not have been much of a room, but was apparently sufficiently large for the prophet to pray and meditate and have a bed on which he could stretch himself. Having a house with more than a single room may signify that her circumstances had once been much better, that the death of her husband, the famine, or both had resulted in the penurious situation in which Elijah found her.

Just as the Lord had spiritually prepared Elijah to meet the widow, he surely spiritually prepared her for the coming encounter as well. Due to this preparation and the general nature of Near Eastern hospitality, it is not too surprising that, when Elijah arrived at the gate of the city and asked the widow for a little water to drink, she went "to fetch it" (1 Kings 17:10–11). What is more surprising is that there was any water to fetch! The famine had extended beyond the borders of Israel to affect this surrounding area as well. The Lord likely sent Elijah to this city because there was still water there. The poor widow's obedient response to Elijah's request reminds us of similar biblical narratives: Abraham's servant, seeking a wife for his master's son Isaac, asked water of a stranger named Rebekah in Nahor (see Genesis 24:10–28); and Jesus requested a drink from a woman at a well in Samaria (see John 4:1–30). The generous response of all three women—the widow, Rebekah, and the Samaritan—in giving water to a stranger is indicative of oriental culture. But in each of these three cases, an additional, greater request was also made, one requiring faith. In the widow's case, it was a specific request for her last morsel of food.

As the widow went for water, Elijah, famished from his journey, called to her, "Bring me, I pray thee, a morsel of bread in thine hand" (1 Kings 17:11). It is easy to imagine her stopping abruptly and turning to him in amazement. A request for a little drink was one thing, but one for food quite another. She responded, "As the Lord thy God liveth, I have not a cake, but an handful of meal in a barrel, and a little oil in a cruse" (1 Kings 17:12). Her response began with a solemn affirmation by her swearing an oath by Elijah's God. What did she know of his God? How specifically had the Lord "commanded" her to prepare for Elijah's coming? (1 Kings 17:9.) It is remarkable that the first recorded phrases of both Elijah and the widow are oaths sworn by the life of Israel's God. The widow's oath affirmed that she had no "cake", meaning already cooked bread, probably somewhat like our flat fry bread. Her larder was entirely empty except for a handful of meal in a barrel—language denoting flour in a pottery jar—and a little olive oil. Divulging the extremity of her circumstances, she indicated she had been "gathering two sticks, that I may go in and dress it for me and my son, that we may eat it, and die" (1 Kings 17:12). Note that she was gathering only two sticks, which would not make much of a fire. Perhaps fuel was very scarce. Or, more likely, she had so little flour and oil that two sticks would make a fire large enough to cook all she had.

Can we imagine what the widow of Zarephath was thinking? She simply had no more food and was about to prepare a final simple meal to share with her son to prolong their lives as much as possible. Elijah understood something of the pangs of hunger and sensed her desperate situation. Yet, with assurance, he said to her, "Fear not; go and do as thou hast said: but make me thereof a little cake" (1 Kings 17:13). Was he asking her to split what little she had three ways instead of two, asking her to abbreviate the short space of mortal life she had left? No, he was asking even more than that, for he said, "Make me thereof a little cake first" (v. 13). For *him* first? Could he really ask such a thing? As a man, he was far more capable of providing for himself in that society than was she. Yet he had said, "Make me thereof a little cake first, and bring it unto me, and after make for thee and for thy son" (v. 13). But if she made even a little bread for him, there would be nothing left for her and her son. Was he being supremely selfish? What did he expect? What did he really want? And what must the poor widow have wondered?

Then came from Elijah's lips the glorious promise, "For thus saith the Lord God of Israel, The barrel of meal shall not waste, neither shall the cruse of oil fail, until the day that the Lord sendeth rain upon the earth" (1 Kings 17:14). Suddenly, the whole picture became complete; he had not been asking how much food she had, but how much faith. He was asking not just for her surplus but whether she was willing to give the proverbial widow's mite, "all that she had" (Mark 12:44). What can we make of her reaction to Elijah's request? Was it fear generated by the commanding presence of this stranger? Was she taking her chances against the odds, simply wistful wishing, or was it something more? Definitely more. There is no record of any verbal retort from her to the prophet's request, but, exhibiting faith in the power and promise of God's prophet, she simply "went and did according to the saying of Elijah" (1 Kings 17:15). What greater tribute could be paid to any of us than the one paid to the widow, that she "went and did"? This demonstration of her faith in action resulted in a rich reward, for "she, and he, and her house, did eat many days. And the barrel of meal wasted not, neither did the cruse of oil fail, according to the word of the Lord, which he spake by Elijah." (1 Kings 17:15–16.)

Notice that although Elijah spoke the words, the promise came from the Lord. The Lord's promises never fail. In the preface to the Doctrine and Covenants, the Lord said: "Search these commandments, for they are true and faithful, and the prophecies and promises which are in them shall all be fulfilled. What I the Lord have spoken, I have spoken, and I excuse not myself; and though the heavens and the earth pass away, my word shall not pass away, but shall all be fulfilled, *whether by mine own voice or by the voice of my servants, it is the same.*" (D&C 1:37–38; italics added.) Just as the Lord's promise through his prophet worked a miracle in the widow's life, so miracles can be experienced in our lives today as we heed the Lord's servants. What greater blessings could we ever seek than those tailored as specifically to our needs as the barrel of meal and cruse of oil were to hers? Sometimes we think our circumstances so extreme as to be impossible of resolution. Would the Lord do any less for us than he did for the widow long ago? Does he have any less love for us? No, he promises and he fulfills, for he is "the same yesterday, today, and forever" (Mormon 9:9).

There is, however, one warning regarding our expectation of blessings. It is that "God will give liberally to him that asketh . . . if [he] ask not amiss" (2 Nephi 4:35). In his New Testament epistle, James warned, "Ye ask, and receive not, because ye ask amiss, that ye may consume it upon your lusts" (James 4:3). We should learn to be satisfied with and grateful for the Lord's helping us meet our needs. Notice how he first tried the widow's faith, then blessed her with enough for her daily needs, but not with a surplus. Likewise, Jehovah required the children of Israel in the wilderness to gather manna each day except for the seventh day, the mandated day of rest. Was the sending of manna any less a miracle because they had to work, gathering it each day? Are there not times when he gives each of us just what we need without any excess and when receiving even that depends on our working and striving for it? We should not read into this story, as some have done, that we can do a good deed and the Lord will provide for us thereafter without any effort or concern on our part. The Lord does not operate in that way. Even the widow had not seen the end of her trials.

"And it came to pass after these things, that the son of the woman, the mistress of the house, fell sick; and his sickness was so sore, that there was no breath left in him" (1 Kings 17:17). The text fails to explain exactly what happened to her son. Some biblical commentators who profess to believe in the scriptural record have nonetheless expressed their doubt that the child was really dead.[1] However, the reference to "breath" in "no breath left" must have been used by the author of 1 Kings in the same context as "the breath of life" in Genesis 2:7. The use of the words *slay* (v. 18) and *slaying* (v. 20) by the widow and Elijah, respectively, presupposes the death of the child. Therefore, there seems to be no reason to interpret this verse as indicating something other than that the child had died.

Notice the widow's reaction to this tragedy as she spoke to Elijah: "What have I to do with thee, O thou man of God? art thou come unto me to call my sin to remembrance, and to slay my son?" (1 Kings 17:18.) A careful reading of her response indicates that she did not blame Elijah for her son's death as much as herself. Perhaps some secret, hidden sin from her past resurfaced in her feelings, filling her with grief. Or maybe Elijah's righteousness prompted her to perceive her general unworthiness. Such feelings are reminiscent of Peter's exclamation to the Master, "Depart from me; for I am a sinful man, O Lord" (Luke 5:8). In any case, her sense of guilt caused her to turn inward with an accusatory attitude. Had she instead blamed someone or something other than herself for this calamity, it is to be wondered if the Lord would have blessed her with the miracle Elijah would soon perform. Godly sorrow for sin produces miracles, both spiritual healing and restoration of life. Note that humble people usually look inward for the source of their problems instead of abandoning personal responsibility and seeking to place blame elsewhere. It is surprising to many students of the scriptures to realize that the inspired leaders of the Nephites in the Book of Mormon never attributed the problems of their people to the Lamanites, but to the sins and omissions of the Nephites themselves (see Alma 59:11–12; Helaman 12:2, 4–6; 3 Nephi 3:15–16). Their prophetic writings reflect the attitude that many of our calamities are self-generated. They understood that with agency comes responsibility for our own actions and attitudes, that eventually we will reap what we sow.

Elijah took the child's body from its mother, carried it to the solitude of his room, laid it upon his own bed, and then poured out his soul in prayer. He did not attempt to explain to the widow why her son had died. He probably did not know. Nor did he speculate about it. He himself may have had questions about why the boy died. Instead of talking or asking, he acted, providing a powerful example for us today. Sometimes, when confronted with a difficulty, we sit and discuss it at length: Why am I in this situation? What brought this about? What should have happened differently? Who is at fault here? There is much of a "talk show mentality" in our culture, evidenced by people wanting to endlessly talk about their problems. Instead of constantly wondering and waiting, thinking and talking—or talking without thinking—debating and arguing, why not be up and about, resolving the situation? Instead of praying, "Why me?" why not plead instead, "Lord, help me!" That is essentially what Elijah did. Why Elijah stretched himself upon the child three times is unknown, though the prophet Elisha did something similar. More detail is given in the account about Elisha found in 2 Kings 4:32–35, but we still do not understand what exactly was being done, nor why. The Lord responded to Elijah's prayer: "And the Lord heard the voice of Elijah; and the soul of the child came into him again, and he revived" (1 Kings 17:22). The widow must surely have rejoiced at the return of her son. This miraculous event certainly confirmed Elijah's divine authority, and the fact that "the word of the Lord in [his] mouth [was] truth" (1 Kings 17:24). With that verse, we conclude the recorded events of Elijah's experiences with the widow of Zarephath. Why had the Lord brought Elijah to this city? For safety and sustenance? Yes, but also to test, strengthen, and confirm the widow's faith.

What other lessons can be gleaned from 1 Kings 17? Like many others recorded in scripture, the miracle that perpetuated the meal and oil defies an explanation based on known science. Miracles are manifestations of the power of God, not events contrary to nature as some have described them. Indeed, it is nature's God who is performing them, using some higher law which we do not now understand. This chapter shows Jehovah's power over those elements that direct weather patterns, expand the supply of foodstuffs, and control life itself.

We do well to pay attention to the favorable portrayal of the widow. Remember that she is a Gentile, that is to say, not a descendant of Jacob, the father of the house of Israel. She is gracious and hospitable, humble enough to feel pangs of guilt for sin, and sufficiently spiritually perceptive to recognize Elijah as a man of God. In Jesus' day the Jews seem to have forgotten that the widow was a Gentile until he reminded them at the synagogue in Nazareth (see Luke 4:24–26). There the Lord referred to her as part of his proof that "no prophet is accepted in his own country" (Luke 4:24). Elijah's going to the gentile widow after being re- jected within Israel further symbolizes the gospel going to the Gentiles after its rejection by most of the Jews in the meridian of time. Jesus told his followers when he healed the servant of a cen- turion, a Gentile, "Verily I say unto you, I have not found so great faith, no, not in Israel. And I say unto you, That many shall come from the east and west, and shall sit down with Abraham, and Isaac, and Jacob, in the kingdom of heaven." (Matthew 8:10–11.)

Why are these few specific events recorded about Elijah? There must be great significance to each act and each word. Remember that Elijah follows and mirrors Moses, and precedes and prefigures Christ. Just as the miracle of the meal and oil foreshadowed the miracles of the loaves and fishes in Jesus' ministry, the circum- stances surrounding the raising of the widow's son present Elijah as a type of the Savior. Why did the widow's son die? We cannot say. However, we remember the Lord's response to his disciples, ex- plaining why a man had been born blind: "that the works of God should be made manifest in him" (John 9:3). Also, when told about the sickness of his friend Lazarus, the Savior replied that it was "for the glory of God" (John 11:4). So although we do not know why the widow's son died, we can understand the importance of his being raised from the dead: it manifested the power of God in an- swer to a widow's faith and demonstrated the existence of priest- hood power and authority held by the prophet. It also stands as a type or foreshadowing of Jesus' raising of another widow's only son, the son of the widow of Nain (see Luke 7: 11–16). And if, as we suppose, Mary, the mother of Jesus, became a widow at a fairly early age, was not the miracle performed by Elijah in that small upper loft in Zarephath a foreshadowing of the raising of her Son, as well?

Chapter Four

THE MEETING OF PROPHET
AND KING

CHAPTER 18 OF 1 KINGS BEGINS: "AND it came to pass after many days, that the word of the Lord came to Elijah in the third year." The exact meaning of the phrase "in the third year" remains unclear. It has been understood by some scholars to mean one full year plus parts of the previous and following years. That would make the duration of the famine just over one year, perhaps fourteen to eighteen months.[1] This interpretation would coincide with the ancient chronicles that mention a famine of one year during the reign of King Ethbaal of Tyre.[2]

However, the New Testament's two references to the famine, one by the Savior and one in the Epistle of James, both record the duration of the drought as three and one-half years (see Luke 4:25; James 5:17). Certain commentators have sought to discount such a lengthy dry period because of the devastation it would cause in an already arid region. They attribute those references to the rabbinic tradition, which says that the number three and one-half, being half of the sacred number seven, represents a mystic cycle of disaster.[3] Others suggest that the number three and one-half in rabbinic literature is not a specific number of years and months but rather a phrase meaning "a period" or "a duration" of time, much like the phrase "after many days" in 1 Kings 18:1.[4]

Thus we cannot specify the exact length of the drought any more than we can determine how long the prophet spent in Zarephath, or how long he was at Cherith. However long the precise duration of the famine, Elijah had undoubtedly been awaiting the Lord's next directive. Whereas the word of the Lord to him had previously been "hide thyself" (1 Kings 17:3), it was now "shew thyself" (1 Kings 18:1). And to whom? To King Ahab, no less. Why? Because the Lord was about to send rain upon the earth.

If ever there was a time when Ahab and his people should have been brought to the depths of humility, it should have been at that moment. The heavens had been sealed for long enough that "there was a sore famine in Samaria" (1 Kings 18:2). We can only imagine the suffering, the complaints to the king, and the demands for relief. Yet, when we next encounter Ahab, what was he doing? Looking for any remaining scrubby fodder for his horses and mules. If, as it appears, the king had some right to the first crop of the year (see Amos 7:1), he was probably searching for grass on the supposition that his animals were the most important in the kingdom, and whatever growth might remain should be his. We cannot help but wonder if he was as concerned about his subjects as he apparently was about maintaining the royal animals. Note that we find him looking down for grass when he should have been looking up to heaven for forgiveness.

Ahab was on this scouting expedition for forage with his steward, Obadiah—not to be confused with the Old Testament prophet of the same name. The name Obadiah translates into "servant of the Lord." The text tells us that this servant "feared the Lord greatly: for it was so, when Jezebel cut off the prophets of the Lord, that Obadiah took an hundred prophets, and hid them by fifty in a cave, and fed them with bread and water" (1 Kings 18:3–4). The term *prophets* here probably means those who had a witness that Jehovah was the living God of Israel and served him. This persecution of the prophets by Jezebel, which has not previously been mentioned in the text, most likely took place during

Elijah's absence from the country, possibly in retaliation for the famine. Ahab suggested to Obadiah that they take different paths to look for grass, the temporal reflecting the spiritual, for the two of them were already wandering different spiritual paths. Appropriately, Obadiah's path, like his faith and course of life, would lead him to the Lord's mouthpiece. Ahab would find nothing.

"And as Obadiah was in the way, behold, Elijah met him: and he knew him, and fell on his face, and said, Art thou that my lord Elijah?" (1 Kings 18:7.) This verse and the next seem contradictory. Was Obadiah asking if this was Elijah or was he exclaiming in surprise that it was Elijah? His first word, "Art," is in italics, which means that it was added by the King James translators in an attempt to clarify the meaning of the sentence, which lacked that word in the original Hebrew. Without the word "Art," it seems Obadiah was making a declaration. Did he perhaps recognize Elijah by his clothing, by the mantle the prophet wore, or from someone else's description? Or had he perhaps seen Elijah before so that he knew him already? It is difficult to discern which is correct. In either case, Elijah confirmed his identity. He then instructed the prostrate steward to inform the king that Elijah was there. Obadiah's immediate response was, "What have I sinned, that thou wouldest deliver thy servant into the hand of Ahab, to slay me?" (1 Kings 18:9.) His fear was probably well founded; for Obadiah to return to Ahab with word that he had seen Elijah without capturing or killing him would likely have caused Ahab to fly into a rage, resulting in the forfeiture of Obadiah's life.

The king's servant then related, "As the Lord thy God liveth, there is no nation or kingdom, whither my lord hath not sent to seek thee" (1 Kings 18:10). Note that Obadiah begins with an oath, the same one used by the widow of Zarephath, referring to "thy God." It appears that the only ones in the narrative who had not recognized that Elijah was a messenger from God were Ahab and Jezebel! We infer from Obadiah's statement that Ahab had sent into all neighboring kingdoms searching for Elijah, either to convince the prophet to reverse the curse or to destroy him. Indeed Ahab required their rulers to search their territories and take an oath that Elijah was not there. Yet, for the majority of the time Ahab sought him, the prophet was safely housed within Jezebel's own father's domain. Maybe that is one place Ahab had not even thought to check.

In such an abbreviated narrative, Obadiah's explanation of why he was so hesitant to follow Elijah's command seems extraordinarily long. Perhaps Obadiah had some part in recording the events now found in the book of 1 Kings. In any event, the steward detailed the source of his fears and pleaded for exemption from the task as reward for his action in hiding the prophets. Elijah, to assure the doubting suppliant, again used an oath to seal his word: "As the Lord of hosts liveth, before whom I stand, I will surely shew myself unto him to day" (1 Kings 18:15). This oath is identical to the one with which Elijah introduced himself to Ahab except for the substitution of the phrase "Lord of hosts" for "Lord God of Israel." The most frequent use of the word *hosts* in the Old Testament is in reference to the multitudes that make up an army. But it also carries the connotation of all created life, as in Genesis 2:1, "Thus the heavens and the earth were finished, and all the host of them." Elijah's God is both the leader of the armies of Israel and the creator of all things. Having heard this solemn oath in the name and by the life of that being whom he also worshiped, Obadiah "went to meet Ahab, and told him" (1 Kings 18:16).

We then read that "Ahab went to meet Elijah" (1 Kings 18:16) and that, when he saw him, he said, "Art thou he that troubleth Israel?" (v. 17.) Ahab's comment reflects his belief that the cause of the drought had been Elijah's effrontery and defiance, which kindled the wrath of Baal. Since the word "Art" is again italicized, indicating it was not in the original Hebrew, we are left to wonder if this was really phrased as a question, perhaps a sarcastic one, or as an accusation, "Thou art he that troubleth Israel." In either case, Elijah's response turned the pointed jab back at the king: "I have not troubled Israel; but thou, and thy father's house, in that ye have forsaken the commandments of the Lord, and thou hast followed Baalim" (v. 18). Elijah condemned not only Ahab but all his father's descendants, meaning the extended family of Omri. Baalim is the plural form of Baal, denoting false gods in general.

Note that both the widow of Zarephath and Obadiah, when

confronted with a dilemma, essentially said, "What sin have I committed that such and such should happen?" They both looked inward for the ultimate source of their problems, even though they may not have been at fault at all. Ahab, on the other hand, with so many sins to his credit, blamed Elijah for Israel's distress. Oh, how blind to the truth are the wicked! They blame everyone for their problems except themselves. Ahab's words are reminiscent of those of Laman and Lemuel murmuring against Nephi: "Our younger brother thinks to rule over us; and we have had much trial because of him" (2 Nephi 5:3). How remarkably different these records would be if they had been written by Laman or Ahab rather than by the prophets of God!

Elijah then issued his challenge, "Now therefore send, and gather to me all Israel unto mount Carmel, and the prophets of Baal four hundred and fifty, and the prophets of the groves four hundred, which eat at Jezebel's table" (1 Kings 18:19). Elijah wanted the entire covenant people to be present to witness his challenge to the false god. The way the text reads, it sounds as though the king worshiped Baal and the queen worshiped Asherah. Elijah requested eight hundred and fifty prophets, yet the balance of chapter 18 refers only to the four hundred and fifty of Baal. Either the others were there and simply not mentioned, or Jezebel's prophet-priests did not attend the contest on Mount Carmel. Sometime after that event, Ahab gathered four hundred prophets to give him counsel about a battle (see 1 Kings 22:6). Since the priests at Carmel were apparently all killed, perhaps the four hundred referred to in chapter 22 were the priests of Jezebel who did not attend the rites at Carmel; either that or Ahab installed a large number of new ones. The phrase "which eat at Jezebel's table" indicates state-supported religion. Jezebel not only introduced priestcraft and apostasy but also subsidized it from the tax revenues taken from the supposed followers of Jehovah.

The text fails to provide further surrounding details of the meeting between Ahab and Elijah. The where, when, and how are glossed over so that we can move quickly to the confrontation on Carmel. The name *Carmel* means orchard, vineyard, garden, or fertile place. It is always written in the Hebrew text with the defi-

nite article *the*, making it *the Carmel*, or the garden place. Carmel
stood on the border between the kingdom of Israel and the kingdom of Tyre, and had probably come under Israelite control during
the military exploits of King David. The fact that the altar of
Jehovah on Carmel had been broken down may mean that the area
had been reconquered by Baal's followers. Perhaps this was done by
the Baal priests as a demonstration or assertion of their supremacy
as they passed this area on their way to accept the invitation of
Jezebel to join her in Samaria. Being on the border of the two lands
put Elijah on a pinnacle between the territories supposedly gov-
erned by the two opposing gods, an ideal spot for a contest. It may
have been considered neutral ground, or it may have been chosen
by Elijah as a location intended to give the priests of Baal every
added advantage, so that the demonstration of the God of Israel's
power might be even more impressive.

Mount Carmel is not a single peak but a long range of hills ex-
tending several miles in a southeasterly direction from the shores
of the Mediterranean Sea near the modern port city of Haifa. On
its heights, one can overlook the Mediterranean Sea to the west
and the fertile valleys and forested mountains of northern Israel to
the east. While it is not possible to place the exact location of
Elijah's encounter with the priests of Baal, a site that well fits all
the parameters outlined in the text is a place known today as El
Muhrakah on the southern end of the Carmel range. While studying this episode, it is useful to try to visualize the spot. The following provides a helpful description of the area:

> At the eastern extremity of the ridge, where the wooded heights
> of Carmel sink down into the usual bleakness of the hills of
> Palestine, is a terrace of natural rock. It is encompassed by dense
> thickets of evergreens; and upon it are the remains of an old and
> massive square structure, built of large hewed stones. This is el-
> Muhrakah; and here, in all probability, stood Elijah's altar (1 Kings
> 18:30). The situation and environs answer in every particular to the
> various incidents of the narrative. A short distance from the terrace
> is a fountain, whence the water may have been brought which was
> poured round Elijah's sacrifice and altar (chap. 18:38). The terrace
> commands a noble view over the whole plain of Esdraelon, from the

banks of the Kishon down at the bottom of the steep declivity, away to the distant hill of Gilboa, at whose base stood the royal city of Jezreel. . . . On the lower declivities of the mountain is a mound called Tell el-Kusis, "the Hill of the Priests," which probably marks the very scene of the execution. May not the present name of the Kishon itself have originated in this tragic event—it is called Nahr el-Mokatta, "the River of Slaughter." The prophet went up again to the altar, which is near, but not upon, the summit of the mountain. While he prayed, he said to his servant, "Go up now, look toward the sea." The sea is not visible from the terrace, but a few minutes' ascent leads to a peak which commands its whole expanse. . . . The modern name of the whole range of Carmel is Jebel Mar Elias, "the mountain of St. Elijah."[5]

And thus the stage was set for the great confrontation. "So Ahab sent unto all the children of Israel, and gathered the prophets together unto mount Carmel" (1 Kings 18:20). All was in readiness for the vindication of "the Lord God of Israel" (1 Kings 17:1).

Chapter Five

THE
CHALLENGE

THE PEOPLE OF AHAB'S KINGDOM FELT they had a special relationship with the God of Israel. Approximately a millennium earlier, the Lord Jehovah had made a sacred covenant with their ancestor Abraham. In exchange for obedience to all the commands
of God, Abraham received the promise of a numerous posterity,
lands of inheritance, and the power to act in the name of God,
known as the holy priesthood. Abraham was also promised that the
Messiah would come through his lineage. (See Genesis 17:1–8;
Abraham 2:8–11.) This sacred covenant was renewed with Abraham's son Isaac and grandson Jacob (see Genesis 26:3–5, 24;
28:13–15). The Lord even changed Jacob's name to Israel (see
Genesis 32:27–28) and blessed him with twelve sons who became
the heads of the twelve tribes of Israel, ten of which would later
constitute the kingdom of Ahab. Following Jacob's death, the
tribes of Israel sojourned in Egypt, where they were enslaved. The
Lord freed them miraculously, gathered them under the leadership
of Moses, and led them through the wilderness to Mount Sinai.
There the Lord sought to renew with the people the covenant
given to their fathers and promised them, "Now therefore, if ye
will obey my voice indeed, and keep my covenant, then ye shall be

a peculiar treasure unto me above all people: for all the earth is mine: and ye shall be unto me a kingdom of priests, and an holy nation" (Exodus 19:5–6).

The tribes of Israel eventually settled in the land called Canaan, the territory which was later split into the kingdoms of Israel and Judah. During the next several hundred years, they lived in varying states of adherence to the commandments of God. For many, remembrance of the covenant wore thin. The abominations of Jeroboam and his successors in the kingdom of Israel had weakened what residual understanding they had of what the covenant relationship meant. They had fallen into the easy trap of forgetting that being a "chosen people" meant they were *chosen* to do something, namely to be the bearers of the Lord's power and blessings to all peoples. Being *chosen* does not indicate a given people's importance reflected by the choice of God, but rather the choice of that people to be a reflection of God's preeminence. Rather than understanding what it meant to be *chosen*, they began to think that they were simply *choice*.

As if this spiritual drifting were not enough of a hindrance to their ability to fulfill their divine mandate, the nation of Israel then had Ahab for a king. Even taking the most positive view of Ahab, he could at best be considered a compromiser, for he had compromised the covenant with Jehovah by intermingling with it the trappings of Baal worship. Yet, then as well as now, it is not compromise but courage that brings forth the blessings of heaven.[1] Courage springs from purity and makes its possessor fearless. As the writer of Proverbs said, "The righteous are bold as a lion" (28:1). With all of Israel vacillating, the Lord needed a lion. He sent Elijah. The confrontation on Carmel between the prophet and the king would prove to gathered Israel who had true courage and who had been compromised.

As the crowds climbed to the appointed place atop Mount Carmel, Elijah watched them come, pondering and praying as he did so. A diverse assembly gathered to view the remarkable contest. On the hill, hundreds of Baal's priests, arrayed in their long robes of fine linen, milled and chanted. The king, accompanied by many from his court, sat prominently on a dais under a canopy with a cover over his head to protect him from the blazing sun. Surrounding them, the multitudes of Israel, who had come at the king's bidding, mingled, chatted, and wondered what all this signified. In the midst of them all, Elijah stood alone. Or did he? Were there not unseen angels surrounding and protecting him? Was not all heaven arrayed behind him? Can one ever be alone when he is on the Lord's errand?

When the hilltop was filled, the throng waited anxiously to see what Elijah would do or say. What would his proposition be? Why had he gathered them? At length, he turned to the gathered multitude, addressing them instead of the king and his priests. His strong voice carried over the silent throng as he posed the penetrating question: "How long halt ye between two opinions?" Then in equally vibrant tones, he proclaimed his challenge, the only sensible resolution to his question: "If the Lord be God, follow him; but if Baal, then follow him." (1 Kings 18:21.) And what was the response of the multitude to his invitation? "The people answered him not a word" (v. 21).

What did his question mean? Why was the crowd hushed to silence? The word *halt* in verse 21 is translated in many ways, depending on the language or the version of the Bible used. In Hebrew, the word means "to hop," connoting a jumping about in a limping fashion. The same Hebrew verb is used in 1 Kings 18:26, where the priests of Baal hop about their altar. There it might be understood as meaning a ritual dance that would have been part of their priestly ceremonies. Perhaps, then, Elijah's question really asked them, "How long will you try to do the dance of Baal and the dance of Jehovah at the same time?" The Hebrew word at the end of the question—translated "opinions" in the King James Version—has one of two very different meanings. One refers to thoughts or opinions, while the other suggests something forked, like a branch. With all these possibilities, consider the following variant readings:

How long will you straddle the issue?[2]
How long will you sit on the fence?[3]
"How long," he said, "do you mean to hobble first on one leg then on the other?"[4]

> How long will you waver between two opinions?[5]
> How long will you hobble on two crutches?[6]
> How long hop ye about upon two boughs?[7]
> How long are you going to live in two camps at once?[8]

To paraphrase, the general sense of the question seems to have been "How long can you simultaneously serve two masters?"

This confrontation closely mirrored the respective contests between Moses and the Egyptian magicians and Joseph and the diviners of Pharaoh. Simply put, it was a contest of supremacy. Perhaps for the first time, the people realized what the issue really was. They were stunned and silent as though it had not occurred to them that the two ways, following Jehovah and following Baal, were incompatible.

The silence that followed Elijah's challenge must have been somewhat like the stunned silence that reigns over a congregation in a stake conference when a General Authority condemns as evil, or tending toward evil, some worldly pastime we have grown to enjoy. Having been lulled into a false sense of security, we remain temporarily blinded from seeing the logical conclusion of our worldly choice until suddenly—and sometimes forcefully—confronted openly by its true significance. As the reality of what we have been doing and where it will lead sets in, we are moved to silent reflection. If we are humble and receptive, the confirming impression of the Spirit bears witness that we must change our choice or suffer the unhappy consequence. Unfortunately, some fall silent because their irritation rises—irritation that someone, even one with special authority, should question their fixed certitudes. It seems that the "natural man" part of our human nature often leads us to question whether a prophet is truly a prophet when he asks us to do something we do not wish to do, or to change an attitude or action with which we have become comfortable. When truth is presented we are either drawn to its light or offended by its brightness. Hence, the reference to the word of God as a "two-edged sword" (D&C 6:2). The truth will continue to stand regardless of how we respond, but our response to it surely measures the light and truth within us.

Basically, the multitude gathered upon the hills around Elijah wanted it both ways. They were much like those in today's society who feel that some compromise with the world is necessary in order to remain "modern." Just as Elijah's words indicated to the ancient Israelites that it was necessary to choose one or the other, so have the Lord's current spokesmen taught that the two paths cannot be blended or compromised, that we are to live in the world but not be of the world. The one path is exceedingly crooked; the other perfectly straight.

To another group attracted by the enticements of the world and thereby growing spiritually hardened, Samuel the Lamanite declared, "Ye have sought all the days of your lives for that which ye could not obtain; and ye have sought for happiness in doing iniquity, which thing is contrary to the nature of that righteousness which is in our great and Eternal Head" (Helaman 13:38). Elijah's listeners were hopping or limping because of the unevenness of trying to walk with one foot in the world, following the allure of Baal, and the other foot in the Lord's way. Perhaps their silence indicated they had not grasped the issue as being so clear cut.

It is significant that the Book of Mormon authors teach in opposites—good versus evil, light versus dark, life versus death. Some have jokingly complained that it seems hardly fair for the Lord to paint everything so black and white and then send us to live in a gray world. But that is the point! This life is a test. The Spirit, scriptures, and prophets instruct us to grasp the iron rod that we might successfully find our way through the gray mists. The Lord has assured us there is a way to discern good from evil. The key is given in a sermon by Mormon:

> For behold, my brethren, it is given unto you to judge, that ye may know good from evil; and the way to judge is as plain, that ye may know with a perfect knowledge, as the daylight is from the dark night.
>
> For behold, the Spirit of Christ is given to every man, that he may know good from evil; wherefore, I show unto you the way to judge; for every thing which inviteth to do good, and to persuade to believe in Christ, is sent forth by the power and gift of Christ; wherefore ye may know with a perfect knowledge it is of God.

But whatsoever thing persuadeth men to do evil, and believe not in Christ, and deny him, and serve not God, then ye may know with a perfect knowledge it is of the devil. (Moroni 7:15–17.)

As Mormon taught, there is a gift from God, a light within each of us, that enables us to discern the difference between good and evil, between following the Lord and following Baal. Unless we extinguish that light, it will allow us to find our way through those gray mists. Amazingly, the farther we travel by the glow of its beam, the brighter it grows, making it easier to distinguish the light from the dark. Eventually, this discerning light becomes almost laser-like in its power, infusing all around us with a deeper clarity and contrast. We then truly start to see things "as they really are" (Jacob 4:13).

Elijah sensed that his people had all but smothered that light or Spirit of Christ, leaving nothing more than a smoldering ember. He was calling on them to look inward, to see if they could not fan into flame that tiny spark flickering within each of them. There, on Carmel, the Lord transformed Elijah into a beacon, channeling divine light to his misguided people, to draw them back to the covenant. Elijah offered them the opportunity to rekindle their lights by reigniting them from his; for assuredly, as Elijah stood atop the mount and issued his call to accountability, he proclaimed to all the people, as would Jeremiah at a later time, that God's "word was in mine heart as a burning fire shut up in my bones" (Jeremiah 20:9).

Chapter Six

THE
PREPARATION

HAVING ISSUED THE CHALLENGE, "IF THE Lord be God, follow him," Elijah stood poised for the encounter to begin. Again addressing the people, he stipulated the nature of the contest: "I, even I only, remain a prophet of the Lord; but Baal's prophets are four hundred and fifty men. Let them therefore give us two bullocks; and let them choose one bullock for themselves, and cut it in pieces, and lay it on wood, and put no fire under: and I will dress the other bullock, and lay it on wood, and put no fire under: and call ye on the name of your gods, and I will call on the name of the Lord: and the God that answereth by fire, let him be God. And all the people answered and said, It is well spoken." (1 Kings 18:22–24.)

The issue presented to the people essentially questioned whether Elijah had offended Baal or whether the Canaanite god existed at all. One of the ancient writings known as the Ras Shamra texts boasts of Baal's supposed power over the elements:

> Moreover Baal will send abundance of his rain,
> Abundance of moisture with snow;
> He will utter his voice in the clouds,
> (He will send) his flashing to the earth with lightning.[1]

If Baal was truly this powerful god of weather, why had there been no rain for so long? Elijah's contest thus challenged Baal to prove his divinity and show himself by sending fire to burn a sacrifice offered to him. The use of fire as the sign was a specially chosen witness of divinity, for the god who could bring fire from heaven to the altar was the one who controlled lightning, and whoever could produce lightning could also produce rain to end the drought.

Elijah gave every possible advantage to his opponents. He met them on a hilltop over which their god claimed dominion. The sea, the source of moisture that Baal supposedly controlled, was nearby, providing a ready resource for the god of rain. The summit of the mountain itself put them all closer to heaven and made it easier for a firebolt to reach them. Elijah pointed out to the people the staggering odds: "I, even I only, remain a prophet of the Lord; but Baal's prophets are four hundred and fifty men." Elijah then addressed the priests of Baal, "Choose you one bullock for yourselves, and dress it first; for ye are many; and call on the name of your gods, but put no fire under" (1 Kings 18:25). He also let them go first, readying their sacrificial bull on the altar of Baal, which appears to have already been in existence at that location. Elijah afforded the priests all the time they wished. Every advantage was theirs.

Some readers have fretted over how Elijah's parentage and tribal affiliation affected the legitimacy of his offering sacrifice at Carmel. Was Elijah a Levite, of the house of Aaron? We do not know. The Lord obviously put his stamp of approval on Elijah's actions, whatever the prophet's specific lineage. While Elijah lived about midway through the Mosaic dispensation, it is clear to us that at some point Elijah received the holy Melchizedek Priesthood with all its accompanying powers, which would have enabled him to function in the performances of the lesser or Levitical Priesthood. Joseph Smith taught, "All the prophets had the Melchizedek Priesthood."[2] It seems logical that Elijah's ordination to this higher priesthood would have occurred sometime before we first met him in 1 Kings 17:1, since his miracles evidenced such authority, particularly his power in sealing the heavens, which sealing power is held only by those possessing the keys of the Melchizedek Priesthood.

The priests of Baal, dressed in beautiful regalia, bedecked with the insignias of their status, put on a fine show. "They took the bullock which was given them, and they dressed it, and called on the name of Baal from morning even until noon, saying, O Baal, hear us." After a few hours, everyone began to tire. "But there was no voice, nor any that answered." Jewish tradition states that the Lord had commanded all creation to remain completely silent be-cause any sound—the rustling of leaves, the chirping of crickets, the call of birds—would be grasped by the priests as an answer from their god. The world was still.[3] To increase the power of their pleas, the priests "leaped upon the altar which was made." (1 Kings 18:26.) The word *leaped* is the same Hebrew word seen in 1 Kings 18:21 and probably refers to some type of ritual dance on and around the altar to attract the attention of Baal. This was likely the proverbial "rain dance" so common in many cultures. When the chants and prayers did not succeed, the dancing began. As noon came and went and Elijah began to ridicule the priests, the dancing turned to hysteria.

Elijah could remain subdued only so long, as he watched this mockery of true worship. His response to the show of the priests was one of righteous derision. "And it came to pass at noon, that Elijah mocked them, and said, Cry aloud: for he is a god; either he is talking, or he is pursuing, or he is in a journey, or peradventure he sleepeth, and must be awaked" (1 Kings 18:27). Elijah taunted them with allusions to a god too busy to be beckoned by his priests—even four hundred and fifty of them. These insults were even stronger than they seem at first glance. Can one worship a god who likes to take trips and leave the world to run itself with-out supervision? Or a god who is so busy talking that he would not interrupt his chat to respond to the pleas of his ardent followers? The phrase "he is pursuing" actually should read "he has gone aside," which some commentators interpret as a euphemism to mean "he has gone to the bathroom."[4] The taunt about a god who is sleeping should have been particularly significant before the multitudes of Israel, who had in their hymnal a song which poeti-cally confirmed, "Behold, he that keepeth Israel shall neither slumber nor sleep" (Psalm 121:4).

Why did Elijah respond to the ranting of the priests in such a way? It is one thing not to worship a given god; it is something quite different to ridicule and mock him. Remember, though, our discussion about how the Lord paints things black and white. His covenant people seemed unable to sift through the gray without Elijah's exposing the absurdities of what they had been doing. It necessitated his pointing contemptuously at those whose antics had sidetracked so many from the worship of Jehovah. As a general rule, sarcasm has no place in the Lord's kingdom or in our interaction with one another. But under the Lord's inspiration, there are moments when it is used in a divine manner to expose or ridicule evil designs and hearts.

When the Lord gave the parable of the lost sheep and said to the self-righteous Pharisees, "Joy shall be in heaven over one sinner that repenteth, more than over ninety and nine just persons, which need no repentance" (Luke 15:7), he was not saying the *just* were safe on their own; no one is considered *just* or justified under the law alone. Jesus chided their self-righteousness, which they based on their assumption that they could fully keep the law of Moses. Simultaneously, he rebuked their unwillingness to accept him as the Mediator who could extend mercy when the law was broken. In discussing this parable, the Prophet Joseph Smith pointed out that the lost sheep represented "hunting after a few individuals, or one poor publican, which the Pharisees and Sadducees despised."[5] Jesus' essential meaning therefore was "I say unto you, there is joy in the presence of the angels of God over one sinner that repenteth, more than over ninety-and-nine just persons that are so righteous; they will be damned anyhow; you cannot save them."[6] Some have termed such rebuking "divine sarcasm." Suffice it to say, Elijah used a similar technique with the priests of Baal. In so doing, he fulfilled the prophetic utterance of the psalm, "He that sitteth in the heavens shall laugh: the Lord shall have them in derision" (Psalm 2:4).

If great effort and earnest pleading could turn an idol into a real god, the priests of Baal likely would have succeeded. When Elijah began to mock them, they "cried aloud, and cut themselves after their manner with knives and lancets, till the blood gushed out upon them" (1 Kings 18:28). This ritual self-mutilation was a form of perverted sacrifice to their god. The priests' desire to win this contest was so great that they pulled out all the stops. They worked themselves into a raving frenzy, a forced emotional ecstasy, which continued until the time of the evening sacrifice. But the result of all their efforts was that "there was neither voice, nor any to answer, nor any that regarded" (1 Kings 18:29).

One could almost feel sorry for the priests, working so hard for naught. Yet it is truly misplaced zeal to double your speed when you find that you are heading in the wrong direction. Elder Marion G. Romney warned us about enthusiasm for any cause that might lead us in the wrong direction. He said: "We . . . must beware concerning ourselves, that we do not fall into the traps [Satan] lays to rob us of our freedom. We must be careful that we are not led to accept or support in any way any organization, cause, or measure which, in its remotest effect, would jeopardize free agency, whether it be in politics, government, religion, employment, education, or any other field. It is not enough for us to be sincere in what we support. We must be right!"[7] The priests of Baal failed because their assumptions and efforts, even if sincere, were intrinsically wrong. Elijah had the support of heaven because he was right!

As the time of the evening sacrifice approached, it was finally Elijah's turn (see 1 Kings 18:36). It is interesting that that would put Elijah's sacrifice at approximately the same time of day that the descendants of Aaron would have been offering their evening oblation at the great temple in Jerusalem, physically far removed but extremely close spiritually to the events then transpiring on Carmel. According to the Jewish historian Josephus, the preparation of the evening offering would have occurred at about 3 P.M.[8] Speaking to the people for the first time since his challenge early that morning, Elijah invited them, "Come near unto me." He wanted them to approach him closely to see what he was about to do. "And all the people came near unto him. And he repaired the altar of the Lord that was broken down." (1 Kings 18:30.) Elijah's short phrase echoes the Savior's frequent invitation, "Come unto me" (Matthew 11:28; 3 Nephi 30:2). Elijah also wanted the multitude to come spiritually to their God.

Earlier that day, when Elijah challenged the people to follow the true God, he spoke to their faculties of reason by proposing a contest that would appeal to and satisfy their sense of logic. Now, by inviting them to closely observe his reassembly of the stones of the abused and unused altar of Jehovah, he pulled at their hearts. The Lord would confirm the truth to them in the same way that he indicates his will to us, namely, in their minds and in their hearts (see D&C 8:2). Elijah's rebuilding of the altar with twelve stones, one for each of the tribes of Israel, symbolized the restoration of the twelve tribes into one people again, a reuniting and sanctification of a people broken into two kingdoms both by idolatry and by political schism.

Elijah dug a large trench around the altar of the Lord, "put the wood in order, and cut the bullock in pieces, and laid him on the wood" (1 Kings 18:33). He then directed that four barrels—more accurately translated "jars"—of water be poured over the sacrificial animal, wood, and stones. A spring near El Muhrakah on Mount Carmel probably served as the source of the water for filling the jars at that time of drought. Elijah commanded that the jars be filled a second and third time, until the symbolically sacred number of twelve had been reached. Twelve tribes, twelve stones, twelve jars of water. Just as the altar had been complete when the number twelve was reached, so the entire sacrifice was ready when the twelve jars of water had thoroughly soaked the wood and flesh, and even filled the trench around the altar. There is some evidence from antiquity that at times pagan altars were lighted by someone underneath who would start the fire at the appropriate moment to give a spectacular effect to the ceremonies. Elijah's drenching the whole sacrifice with water certified that he was involved in no such trick.

The prophet thus completed all the preparations. He had done all he could do. Having reached his extremity, he was now postured to call upon that Being who alone can accomplish the impossible. Elijah was ready to petition God for a miracle.

Chapter Seven

THE TRIUMPH
AT CARMEL

WITH ALL IN READINESS, ELIJAH positioned himself near the altar in the sight of all the multitude. Everyone's attention followed his upturned eyes and upraised hands as he cried aloud, "Lord God of Abraham, Isaac, and of Israel, let it be known this day that thou art God in Israel, and that I am thy servant, and that I have done all these things at thy word. Hear me, O Lord, hear me, that this people may know that thou art the Lord God, and that thou hast turned their heart back again." (1 Kings 18:36–37.) The Joseph Smith Translation changes the phrase "hast turned their heart" to "mayest turn their heart," clarifying that Elijah was pleading with the Lord to soften the people's hearts and turn them back to Him, instead of declaring what had already been done.

Why did Elijah pray for a miracle? To put the priests of Baal in their place? To demonstrate his own preeminence? No, he desired only that the Lord demonstrate his power so that the people might repent and return to the covenant they had made with Jehovah. The Lord's answer to Elijah's humble plea was immediate. "Then the fire of the Lord fell, and consumed the burnt sacrifice, and the wood, and the stones, and the dust, and licked up the water that was in the trench. And when all the people saw it, they fell on their faces: and they said, The LORD [Jehovah], he is the God; the LORD [Jehovah], he is the God." (Vv. 38–39.) That is to say, they acknowledged Jehovah as God. Elijah's prayer had been answered, both his prayer for fire and for the hearts of the people.

The experience of Elijah at Carmel actually happened just as it is recounted in scripture. It was a historical event. But the happening can also be viewed symbolically. The entire event on Carmel represents the first principles and ordinances of the gospel, namely, faith, repentance, baptism, and the gift of the Holy Ghost. First, Elijah called the people to demonstrate their faith. Asking them, "Whom do you believe?" he called them to follow the true God, to trust in Jehovah. Second, Elijah's reconstruction of the altar that had been broken down was reminiscent of repentance. It symbolized the healing of a broken heart. God's wrath had been kindled by the wickedness of his people. The fire of his indignation must fall either on the people themselves or on their sacrificial substitute. Thus the slain animal laid on the altar was an offering of penance, a symbol of the people's wishing to regain God's favor, a substitute to receive the meting out of justice so that the people might receive mercy instead. Next, the sacrificial offering and the twelve stones of the altar—representing united Israel— were totally immersed in water, symbolic of baptism with its cleansing and purifying connotations. Certain baptisms today are performed over symbols of these same twelve tribes. Lastly, fire, the oft-used symbol of the presence of the Spirit, fell from heaven to consume the entire offering—the animal life (the bullock), the vegetable life (the wood), the stones, the dust (the soil), even the water. The Spirit engulfed everything, calling to mind Joseph Smith's statement that "our God is a consuming fire."[1] Even as fire both consumes and purifies, the multitude before Elijah was renewed. The response of the people was to acknowledge the one true God, the Lord Jehovah.

Additionally, the miracle on Carmel symbolized the atonement of Christ, for, as the Lord has stated, "all things are created and made to bear record of me" (Moses 6:63). In Moses 6:60, he explained, "For by the water ye keep the commandment; by the Spirit ye are justified, and by the blood ye are sanctified." All three of these elements were present at Carmel: the water, the heavenly fire, and the blood of the bullock—a type of the blood of the Lord Jehovah himself. The offering at Carmel thus foreshadowed the future offering of the Holy One of Israel as the sacrificial substitute for the sins of all mankind, including those in attendance at Carmel that day, that he might "purify unto himself a peculiar people, zealous of good works" (Titus 2:14).

The aftermath of the miracle proved to be dramatic. "And Elijah said unto them, Take the prophets of Baal; let not one of them escape. And they took them: and Elijah brought them down to the brook Kishon, and slew them there." (1 Kings 18:40.) Some writers have considered Elijah's killing of the priests of Baal as a disgraceful crime and see regret for having done so as the cause for his sadness reflected in 1 Kings 19:4.[2] Perhaps other readers might acknowledge that difficult times require tough measures, but feel that such actions would be condemned under the New Testament philosophy of "turning the other cheek." Both such explanations seem to miss the mark. We know that the same Lord who gave the Sermon on the Mount also gave the law of Moses (see 3 Nephi 15:4–5), each one being suited to the circumstances of the people at the time. It would seem that Elijah simply implemented the then existing law of Moses, in fulfillment of its provisions requiring the death of all idolaters (see Exodus 22:20; Deuteronomy 13:6–11, 17:2–7).

Elijah then turned his attention to the king, who at that point must have been at least perplexed, if not shocked and dismayed. The prophet said to him, "Get thee up, eat and drink; for there is a sound of abundance of rain" (1 Kings 18:41). Some suppose that all present had been fasting that day because of the nature of the gathering. Perhaps Elijah was mocking Ahab in the sense of "Go, eat and drink after that, if you can." Others have suggested that Elijah invited Ahab to partake of the sacrificial meal.[3] But would Elijah offer to King Ahab that portion of the offering designated by the law of Moses for sustaining the priests? Were there any other priests of Jehovah in attendance? It seems doubtful. Where would Elijah have found a priest after Jezebel's purges? Had he set aside a portion of the sacrifice before placing the remainder on the altar? There was certainly nothing left of the sacrifice after the fire fell; even the stones were gone. Perhaps Elijah was neither castigating the king nor making an invitation but just acknowledging what he knew Ahab would then do: "You can go back now to your eating and drinking and making merry; go back to your hedonistic life." There is no indication of a call to repentance, almost as if Elijah knew such would be fruitless.

The more significant aspect of Elijah's comment to Ahab is that the king had better go or be overtaken by rain. What rain? Where? When? The sky was still absolutely clear, without a cloud in any direction. The humidity continued extremely low, the ground still lay brown and parched as far as eye could see, and the air around them remained hot and motionless. As evening approached, there arose no breeze to refresh them after a long and stressful day. Even though the sun did not blaze as brightly as it had at noonday, it still hung low in the western sky, casting an ashen glow over all creation, as it had for so many evenings for so many months. What rain? Surely Elijah's hearing the sound of abundance of rain was the "hearing of faith" (Galatians 3:2).

"So Ahab went up to eat and to drink. And Elijah went up to the top of Carmel; and he cast himself down upon the earth, and put his face between his knees." (1 Kings 18:42.) Both men were going "up," ascending to their earlier place on the hill from the brook Kishon, where they had just been. But as they went up, their paths separated. One returned to his life of ease and the other went to his knees. In the Book of Mormon, King Benjamin, delivering the words given him by an angel, differentiated between those who remain part of the "natural" world and those who are raised above it by following Christ. He explained: "For the natural man is an enemy to God, and has been from the fall of Adam, and will be, forever and ever, unless he yields to the enticings of the Holy Spirit, and putteth off the natural man and becometh a saint through the atonement of Christ the Lord, and becometh as a child, submissive, meek, humble, patient, full of love, willing to submit to all things which the Lord seeth fit to inflict upon him, even as a child doth submit to his father" (Mosiah 3:19). The different responses of King Ahab and Elijah to all that had happened that day clearly indicate who was still the "natural man" and who was the "saint."

Elijah turned away from the king and toward the Lord. Although the record in 1 Kings 18 does not even specifically state that Elijah was praying, he obviously was. Without doubt, he was offering a prayer of thanksgiving for the Lord's miraculous intervention that day. Also, as might be expected, he was praying for the rain that the Lord had indicated to Elijah he was preparing to send (see 1 Kings 18:1). James 5:18 confirms that Elijah prayed for rain. Likewise, in a letter to some of the brethren in Jackson County, Missouri, after the initial violence there had erupted against them, Joseph Smith wrote, "Hold fast that which you have received. Trust in God. Consider Elijah when he prayed for rain. Go often to your holy places and look for a cloud of light to appear to your help."[4]

Elijah began the day by loudly issuing a challenge to the people and speaking powerfully as God's mouthpiece. In that position, he boldly taunted the raving priests. But when he prayed aloud before the people, asking the Lord to reveal his power, he did so with the humble attitude of a servant, even though he spoke with full voice in order to be heard by all present. Now, when it came time to petition the Lord for rain to end the drought, the multitude had gone. Elijah's voice subsided to a reverent whisper, just as his knees dropped to the ground. Alone, he humbly approached the throne of grace as the spokesman of the people, asking for collective forgiveness and pardon. The difference between those moments when he spoke to the people and those when he spoke with the Lord are remarkable. His changed demeanor depended on his role in relationship to his God. At times he faced the Lord as a suppliant for repentant Israel, while at others he faced the people with the Lord at his side. There is much we can learn from his example. We must ever remember who we are facing and for whom we are speaking in order to keep our words and works in appropriate perspective.

If Elijah then held the sealing power, as we presume he must have, the Lord would have likely promised to temper the elements according to his word. Thus, Elijah meekly approached the Almighty to plead for rain for the parched land and the famished people. He understood that even though the Lord has promised something, that does not exempt us from exerting our most soul-felt and repeated appeals for it. The Lord often waits for us to ask before sending the promised blessing. His doing so reminds us both of his bounteous goodness as the fount of all blessings, and also of our continued, complete dependence on him. Elijah, on his knees that evening so long ago at Carmel—Carmel, remember, means "the garden"—is a type of the Savior on his knees in another garden, the one called Gethsemane. Just as Elijah received no immediate answer to his prayer but had to return to his supplications time and time again, so we read in Luke that Jesus "being in an agony . . . prayed more earnestly" (Luke 22:44). There is a poignant lesson taught by both those prayers, that there are moments of great need when our pleadings must be more intense, filled with more faith than ever before.

Elijah continued praying. Initially, when he sent his servant to check the western sky, there was nothing. But he did not give up. He returned to his prayer and sent his servant again and again. From the heights of Carmel, the servant had a clear view of the Mediterranean, so that any speck of a cloud would be visible on the distant horizon. At last, on the seventh visit to the top of the hill, the servant reported, "Behold, there ariseth a little cloud out of the sea, like a man's hand." A hint of a cloud was enough for Elijah. He sent his servant to Ahab with the message, "Prepare thy chariot, and get thee down, that the rain stop thee not." (1 Kings 18:44.) Even as the message was being delivered and the horses and chariots prepared, "the heaven was black with clouds and wind, and there was a great rain" (v. 45).

Ahab headed speedily for Jezreel, which lay about seventeen miles away, easterly across the plains of Esdraelon. The city straddled Mount Gilboah. The scripture says, "And the hand of the Lord was on Elijah; and he girded up his loins, and ran before Ahab to the entrance of Jezreel" (1 Kings 18:46). A person running on foot can cover a given distance in a relatively straight line more quickly than can an entourage in chariots following roads. But even so, the Lord must have given Elijah mighty strength to reach the city before the king. Until modern times when the plains of Esdraelon were drained, parts thereof were very swampy. When the drought occurred, most of those wetlands probably turned to powdery dust. But with the sudden, heavy rains mentioned in the text, the dust quickly turned to deep mud all along Ahab's route to the city. The chariots carrying him and his attendants were undoubtedly driven with great difficulty, being stuck in the mire, having their wheels break, their horses slipping and falling. Elijah reached the city safely, while Ahab was delayed in the mud. That scenario gives rise to images of a similar scene centuries earlier as Moses reached the eastern shore of the Red Sea safely while the Egyptians following him in chariots "drave them heavily" (Exodus 14:25).

Chapter 18 of 1 Kings closes with the end of the day. Jehovah's power in the eyes of the people had been vindicated. The curse was over, the drought ended. At the close of one of the most memorable days in history, it seems most appropriate that the prophet of God should have reached Jezreel first, being placed geographically, as well as spiritually, "before" the king.

Chapter Eight

THE REVELATION
AT HOREB

ELIJAH HAD NO TIME TO DWELL ON THE triumph at Carmel, for the clouds of rain were quickly followed by clouds of persecution. Immediately upon Ahab's arrival at Jezreel, he "told Jezebel all that Elijah had done, and withal how he had slain all the prophets with the sword" (1 Kings 19:1). Note that Ahab attributed all that happened on that eventful day to Elijah, ignoring the Lord's hand in either the original drought or the new-fallen rain. He was sufficiently hardened that he failed to recognize the hand of God in any of these momentous events. His words set the stage for the conflict between Jezebel, the patroness of Baal, and Elijah. As emissaries of their respective deities, they were poised as archenemies. Their names alone stood in defiance to each other. The literal meaning of Jezebel's name is "Where is the prince? (Baal)" or "Baal is prince," while Elijah's name signifies "Jehovah is my God." Upon learning of the events at Carmel, Jezebel sent a messenger to threaten Elijah's life. "So let the gods do to me, and more also, if I make not thy life as the life of one of them by to morrow about this time" (1 Kings 19:2). And what was Elijah's response? "And when he saw that, he arose, and went for his life, and came to Beer-sheba, which belongeth to Judah, and left his servant there" (v. 3).

Jezebel sought to destroy Elijah, so he fled for his life. Yet a few verses later, Elijah appears depressed and ready to forfeit his life. Something is incongruous here. The Septuagint, an early Greek version of the Old Testament, translates "he saw" in 1 Kings 19:3 as "he feared." While it would be understandable for most of us to fear if our lives were threatened, would Elijah's reaction be the same? Would fear prompt him to flee after all he knew and after all that had happened previously, particularly the immense display of power on Carmel? Was he just succumbing to normal human emotion or was something else involved? Jacob, the father of the tribes of Israel, fled the wrath of his brother Esau, and Moses, the great lawgiver, fled the vengeance of Pharaoh. Perhaps Elijah's flight foreshadowed the child Jesus' fleeing with his family to Egypt to escape Herod the Great's edict of death. But had Elijah fled from fear alone, he could likely have rested in Judah under the protection of righteous King Jehoshaphat. Instead, he went to Beersheba at Judah's southern extremity and then headed south into the wilderness alone.

After all the miraculous manifestations of the Lord's protecting care in Elijah's life, why would he now succumb to fear? Rather than being driven by fear alone, it appears that Elijah was impressed that he needed to journey southward into the wilderness to commune with the Lord. His journey ultimately led him to Mount Horeb, the sacred spot also known as Sinai, where the Lord had established the covenant with the tribes of Israel in the days of Moses. Perhaps Elijah did not know his exact destination until he left his servant at Beersheba and "went a day's journey into the wilderness" (1 Kings 19:4). Beersheba was the last vestige of civilization before entering the desert to the south known as the Negev. Rather than forgetting the Lord and fleeing out of fear, Elijah seems to have entrusted himself to the Lord's safekeeping, knowing that only faith and trust could keep him from being totally alone on this wilderness journey.

Once again, the recorded acts of Elijah's life prefigure those of the Savior while also echoing the experiences of Moses. The Savior would be led into the wilderness by the Spirit to commune with his Father (see JST, Matthew 4:1). Moses was led into the

wilderness of Midian (see Exodus 2:15). As Moses found a bush, so
Elijah found a juniper tree. Though Moses' bush burned while
Elijah's gave shelter from the sun, each of the two great prophets
received divine communication at his respective bush.

Just as human emotions and weakness tempted the Savior
while in the wilderness, nagging feelings of depression tempted
Elijah. As he journeyed southward, first from Jezreel and then from
Beersheba, he had much time to quietly reflect on the momentous
events that had happened of late. He probably felt a certain emotional letdown after the strenuous though exhilarating triumph at
Carmel. The farther he went and the more he pondered on the
lack of commitment of his people—who, even at the very time of
his journey, may have been wandering back to their old ways—the
more depressed he became, almost to the point of despondency.
His reaction resembled that of Nephi, the son of Helaman, who,
following a miraculous vindication of his role as prophet, was
"much cast down because of the wickedness of the people"
(Helaman 10:3). Elijah must have wondered, despite the magnitude of what had happened, whether the conversion of those at
Carmel would last. How could Ahab not recognize the hand of
God? Why is Jezebel still in control? What now of his life? What
good was it to continue if there were none to follow him? Why
live longer?

Elijah steadily sank into an immense internal conflict exagger-
ated by physical and emotional exhaustion. He did not know just
why he must journey to Horeb, but he was impressed that he must
go. However, before he could reach his intended destination, before he could see the light which was sure to appear after his walk
of faith through the darkness, his resolve faltered. He lay down
under the juniper tree and wished it could all end, saying, "It is
enough; now, O Lord, take away my life; for I am not better than
my fathers" (1 Kings 19:4).

Perhaps Elijah was already then fairly elderly, which would help
explain why he said he need not live longer, or perhaps he felt his
mortal mission had ended and he simply wanted to be released,
feeling that he could not go on any longer, that he had nothing
more to offer. His mention of not being better than his fathers may

refer to his spiritual fathers, the earlier prophets, who had likewise been rejected. They had died; why not him? His asking to die showed his acknowledgment that his life was in God's hands, not his own. Elijah's discouragement also mirrors that experienced by Moses when he was discouraged by the hard-heartedness of the people he was called to lead (see Exodus 5:22 and Numbers 11:12–15). Moses had exclaimed, "And if thou deal thus with me, kill me, I pray thee, out of hand, if I have found favour in thy sight; and let me not see my wretchedness" (Numbers 11:15).

Elijah momentarily gave in to a feeling of despair, of wanting to give up. But the Lord had more for Elijah to accomplish. Perhaps the greatest trial of Jesus' mortal mission was the temptation to give up in Gethsemane when the pressure was so great that he literally bled "at every pore" (D&C 19:18). But he held on, hour after agonizing hour, until he could exclaim on the cross, "Father, it is finished, thy will is done" (JST, Matthew 27:54). An angel came to strengthen the Lord in the garden in his time of suffering (see Luke 22:43). Likewise, an angel came to Elijah under the tree to strengthen and encourage him at his lowest moment.

Jezebel had sent a messenger to Elijah with a message of death; the Lord now sent him another messenger with a message of life. As Elijah slept under the tree, "an angel touched him, and said unto him, Arise and eat" (1 Kings 19:5). Elijah arose to find freshly baked bread and water. He ate, drank, and then lay down again, as if the significance of that miraculous meal had been lost on him. In his state of depression, he seems to have viewed it as his last. The angel "came again the second time, and touched him, and said, Arise and eat; because the journey is too great for thee" (1 Kings 19:7). Elijah then knew the Lord would not let him lie there and die. He must go on. So he "arose, and did eat and drink, and went in the strength of that meat forty days and forty nights unto Horeb the mount of God" (1 Kings 19:8). Elijah ate bread and water and subsisted miraculously for forty days, like the forty-day fasts of Moses and Christ. It is significant that Exodus 24:18, referring to Moses, and Matthew 4:2, referring to Christ, both have the identical phrase used in 1 Kings 19:8: "forty days and forty nights." The authors, in each case, wish to convey that this was a total fast, not one just from sunrise to sundown. The bread and water Elijah consumed were certainly more than the common substances that go by the same names; they were heaven sent. Of the three forty-day fasts in scripture, only in the instance of Elijah do we specifically find mention of a preparatory meal of bread and water. It is hard to miss the symbolism that points to the modern sacramental emblems with their attendant promise of eternal life.

"In the strength" of that meal, Elijah made the lonely journey to the sacred mountain, Horeb. "And he came thither unto a cave, and lodged there" (1 Kings 19:9). In Hebrew, the cave on Horeb is referred to as *the* cave, using the definite article, an obvious allusion to the "clift of the rock" (Exodus 33:22) where Moses experienced a supernatural display similar to the one Elijah was about to have. Some interpret the word *lodge* to mean he spent the night and thus infer he was in the cave only one night. However, it seems even more likely that he "lodged" for an extended period, reflecting upon all that had occurred and pondering about the future. Maybe part of the forty days was spent there.

It is easy to envision Elijah struggling within himself. What should he do? Where should he go? Why had he come here? Was he justified in hiding? This period of intense, internal turmoil was inspired by the nagging question which kept coming to his mind, "What doest thou here, Elijah?" As he struggled, the scripture says "the word of the Lord came to him." (1 Kings 19:9.) It most likely came as it comes to all of us who are struggling, with impressions working on our consciences, encouraging us to look inward and prodding us. To maintain his sanity, he may have justified his actions to himself in these terms: "I had to come to save my life. I hoped to be closer to the Lord here. I don't know where to go from here. What does the Lord want me to do next? Have I done all I was supposed to do?" According to scripture, he said, "I have been very jealous for the Lord God of hosts: for the children of Israel have forsaken thy covenant, thrown down thine altars, and slain thy prophets with the sword; and I, even I only, am left; and they seek my life, to take it away" (v. 10).

In the midst of his reflection and prayer, worry and wondering, he was impressed that the Lord was coming and that he should go out to meet him. He went forth with a sense of anxiousness. "At last, an answer to my questions," he must have felt. To his surprise, he was met by dramatic demonstrations of the power of God over the elements of the earth. First, there was an incredible windstorm of such velocity as to break the rocks of the mountains around him. Then came an earthquake to rend and crack the earth to its foundation, causing upheavals of everything the wind had left intact. Next, a great fire consumed all around him. In each case, Elijah simply observed, having seen the manifestations of the Lord's power many times before. Anticipating an encounter with Deity, in each instance he acknowledged the Lord's power but realized that "the Lord was not in the wind . . . the earthquake . . . [nor] the fire" (vv. 11–12).

The experience Elijah was to have on Horeb would not be the "idea" of God or the "essence" of God's power seen in nature. Instead, it would be the revelation of a living, personal Being. During this formidable exhibition, Elijah retreated into the cave to avoid destruction by these upheavals of nature. At that point, the spectacular experience changed. Scripture employs the simple phrase, "And after the fire a still small voice" (v. 12). Elijah had been struggling with the impressions of the Spirit for some time. But now, all the mighty external displays of power aside, there spoke to his innermost self the unmistakable voice of the Spirit, quiet, serene, and peaceful. The miracle of the voice of the Spirit superseded all the miracles of the natural elements he had just witnessed. Verse 13 indicates that Elijah "wrapped his face in his mantle." A general reading of this line leads one to picture Elijah showing great humility and reverence at this momentous occurrence, much like Moses' covering his face out of respect in Exodus 3:16. But perhaps there is even deeper meaning being exhibited by such action.

We can imagine Elijah moving slowly from the darkness where he had taken refuge to the mouth of the cave, a large boulder to his side partly blocking the entrance. As he stepped into the light, both physically and spiritually, the weeks of frustration, wandering, and wondering may have given way to a flood of emotion, mingling sorrow and repentance with surpassing joy. Perhaps he could no longer hold back the fountain of tears. Momentarily overcome, he covered his face with his mantle, not just as a sign of reverence, but also to hide his tears from the Lord. At this moment of great emotional release, in tender, loving tones, the Lord again asked, "What doest thou here, Elijah?" Though the recorded words of Elijah's response are the same as those appearing a few verses earlier, there is an impression that humility and grateful commitment have supplanted the previous sense of excuse and self-justification. The furrowed brow and longing voice implied in verse 10 as Elijah reasoned with himself were replaced by the swollen eyes and tear-stained cheeks of the humble seeker whose prayers are answered. The words of verses 10 and 14 are the same; the feeling and meaning conveyed are worlds apart. Elijah's emotional meeting with the Almighty caused his spirit to be confronted with a clear remembrance of who he was, what the Lord had done through him, and of what else he must yet do. Elijah faced his Maker and, simultaneously, his innermost self.

Earlier, King Ahab had expected a dramatic, external demonstration of the power of Jehovah as proof of Elijah's authority. He received it and ignored it. Elijah, on a higher spiritual plane than Ahab, received a manifestation from deep inside his soul. In Elijah's world, an inharmonious multitude of sounds prevailed: the riotous partying of the wealthy drowned out the agonized pleas of the poor, mocking laughter emanated from the royal court in Samaria, the shouted entreaties from the priests of Baal summoned their god, the sonic blast of a firebolt on Mount Carmel launched the thundering sound of a great "abundance of rain" (I Kings 18:41). Yet, in the midst of such dissonance, Elijah heard and obeyed the most impressive sound of all, the still small voice of the Spirit.

It has been proposed that the somewhat obscure Hebrew phrase rendered as "still small voice" should be translated as "a roaring and thunderous sound."[1] Such a proposal makes no sense in the context of the message contained in chapter 19, nor in light of the Book of Mormon and modern revelation where the phrase is also used and its meaning remains clear (see 1 Nephi 17:45; D&C 85:6). To the contrary, there appears to be great inspiration in the choice of words by the King James translators. The Lord demonstrated to the faithless at Mount Carmel through a dramatic manifestation that he had power over the elements. Although he could, at his command, call the elements to testify of his supremacy, he chose to communicate with his faithful follower through an inward manifestation, a quiet, peaceful voice. Elijah knew then that God at times must resort to calling those otherwise preoccupied, who are dull of hearing, by "the voice of thunderings, and by the voice of lightnings, and by the voice of tempests, and by the voice of earthquakes, and great hailstorms, and by the voice of famines and pestilences of every kind" (D&C 43:25). Elijah also knew that the same Being speaks to his servants by "the voice of his Spirit" (D&C 52:1), that "still small voice, which whispereth through and pierceth all things" (D&C 85:6). Elijah learned, as each of us must, that while it may be far from the loudest voice, the voice of the Spirit is undeniably the strongest and most compelling.

The voice of the Spirit thus led Elijah to his personal encounter with Jehovah. Elijah told the Lord he had been very "jealous" for his sake (1 Kings 19:14). The word might be better translated "zealous," as it is in the Douai Bible and the New International Version, which meaning coincides more with our current usage of the two words. To this expression of loyalty, the Lord responded by assigning Elijah three missions: to anoint a new king of Syria, Hazael; a new king of Israel, Jehu; and a prophetic successor, Elisha. There is no recorded instance of Elijah's personally fulfilling the first two assignments. Either he did so and it was not recorded, or circumstances dictated that he confer such responsibilities on his successor Elisha. In fact, the scriptures tell of Elisha's having done both, either as a confirmation of what Elijah had previously done or in fulfillment of the assignment given him by his prophetic predecessor.

In the course of these assignments, the Lord reassured Elijah that he was not alone in his faithfulness to Jehovah. Just as Joseph Smith, who in a moment similar to Elijah's felt discouraged and abandoned, rejoiced to learn that his friends would stand by him (see D&C 121:9), Elijah must have joyfully received the news that there were yet 7,000 in Israel who had not bowed the knee to Baal (see 1 Kings 19:18). He who had felt so alone was not in reality alone. While the specific number 7,000 may be only symbolic—seven being a sacred Hebrew number denoting perfection or completeness—the realization that there were many who still worshiped the true and living God must have been good news to the prophet. It is also likely that the news reminded Elijah that whatever he was called to pass through, the Lord would be with him. Elijah's trials could never be greater than those that were yet to be borne by the very God he worshiped. In gentle, understanding, and loving tones, would the Lord not have taught and comforted Elijah in words such as these: "Know thou, my son, that all these things shall give thee experience, and shall be for thy good. The Son of Man [shall descend] below them all. Art thou greater than he?" (D&C 122:7–8.)

Some have seen the triumph at Carmel as the high point of Elijah's mortal career. But was not the true high point his communion with the Lord on Horeb? Half a millennium earlier at that sacred place, the Lord confirmed his covenant with his people Israel. Now he confirmed upon Elijah a special responsibility having to do with the continuation and restoration of that covenant. Elijah was assigned to supervise the spiritual future of the covenant people.

Reflect also on the watchful manner by which the Lord brought Elijah to Horeb. The Lord sent ravens to feed him, a widow to supply him with food and lodging during the duration of the famine, an angel to sustain him in his moment of sadness, the voice of the Spirit to encourage and instruct him, and, finally, a visitation from the Lord himself. Faithful obedience to and reliance upon the Lord bring the first Comforter and then ultimately the Second.[2]

Elijah, obedient as ever, left his mountain temple to find and anoint his successor, Elisha, the son of Shaphat. Elijah probably journeyed back through southeastern Judah to the Jordan River and then north along its winding course to the city of Abel-Meholah, Elisha's home. He found Elisha plowing with 12 yoke of oxen. The large number likely indicates Elisha came from a wealthy family. The text makes no specific mention of a holy anointing, but it undoubtedly took place. The only allusion to the choosing and setting apart appears in the phrase, "and Elijah passed by him, and cast his mantle upon him" (1 Kings 19:19).

The first recorded instance of such a mantle or outer cloak being seen as the symbol of a prophet is found in the story of Samuel. His ministry bridged Israel's transition from an era of rule by judges to the reign of kings. When King Saul visited the sorceress of Endor, she supposedly conjured up the spirit of Samuel. When she described the spirit as "an old man . . . covered with a mantle" (1 Samuel 28:14), Saul immediately recognized the description as that of the prophet. It seems possible that a certain type of garment indicated an individual's prophetic calling and that such a custom still existed in Elijah's day. By casting his mantle upon Elisha, Elijah signaled a transference of spiritual power and authority. From this account of the call of Elisha and its sequel at the time of Elijah's translation arose such phrases as "the mantle of the prophet," "the mantle of leadership," "the passing of the mantle."

At the time of his call, Elisha asked if he might return to kiss his father and mother before following the prophet. It is noteworthy that while the Lord had recently told Elijah that there were many who had not *kissed* Baal, Elisha should wish to *kiss* his family as he simultaneously *embraced* the call to the Lord's service. As we shall see, the mission of Elijah is connected very closely with the sacred covenants that bind family members to each other and to the Lord. Elisha's rapid and eager acceptance of his new assignment confirmed the Lord's promise to Elijah that there were many who had not "bowed unto Baal" (1 Kings 19:18). Having said his good-byes and offered sacrifice and thanks, Elisha "arose, and went after Elijah, and ministered unto him" (1 Kings 19:21). Elijah, who so recently felt so alone, now had someone who ministered to him, a counselor, a student, a friend, and someone to whom Elijah would minister with a special charge to prepare him for his own future prophetic role.

Chapter Nine

THE VINEYARD
OF NABOTH

WHILE ELIJAH'S HISTORY PREVAILS AS THE focal point of chapters 17, 18, and 19 of the book of 1 Kings, chapter 20 discusses King Ahab's military encounter with Syria and its consequences. Chapter 21 returns to the narrative concerning the interaction between Elijah and Ahab. The Septuagint has chapter 21 follow 19, indicating its status as a continuation of the Elijah history. Chapter 21 begins with the simple statement that "Naboth the Jezreelite had a vineyard." The significance of this vineyard arose from its location "hard by," or next to, "the palace of Ahab king of Samaria." (1 Kings 21:1.) Note that Ahab is referred to as "king of Samaria," a reference to his capital city, not the kingdom as a whole. Why did he have a palace in Jezreel if his capital was Samaria? Because of Jezreel's location at an elevation of about 375 feet, the king and queen presumably resorted there during the cool winter months to absent themselves from the chilly nights that would prevail in the mountains of Israel, where Samaria stood at 1,340 feet. Jezreel may also have functioned as a secondary place of residence where the king and queen could get away from the center of activity. This might explain why the king took such a personal interest in having a plot of land next door to the palace for a "garden of herbs" (v. 2). Perhaps gardening was a hobby.

Whatever the specific reasons, Ahab approached his neighbor Naboth, saying, "Give me thy vineyard, that I may have it for a garden of herbs, because it is near unto my house: and I will give thee for it a better vineyard than it; or, if it seem good to thee, I will give thee the worth of it in money" (1 Kings 21:2). To us, that sounds like a reasonable request. He offered to either pay for it with cash or give another vineyard of equal or greater value in exchange for it. We do not know if there were other underlying factors involved or pressure tactics being used. It is, therefore, somewhat surprising to read that Naboth declined the offer: "The Lord forbid it me, that I should give the inheritance of my fathers unto thee" (1 Kings 21:3). Perhaps he did not like the king or his queen and so was not inclined to sell his family inheritance. Or maybe there were legal impediments of which we have no knowledge. Or perhaps Naboth was simply content with his circumstances and concerned about a change.

A more probable clue to Naboth's reasoning arises from the fact that, under the law of Moses, property was viewed as hereditary, belonging not only to the owner and his children but also to generations yet unborn (see Leviticus 25:23–28). Property was also viewed as a link to a man's ancestors. The Israelites evidently understood that the land actually belonged to the Lord and that individuals acted only as stewards over it. Under the Mosaic law, it could be mortgaged or sold only with a right of reversion, whereby it would revert to the original owning family in the year of Jubilee (every 50 years). At that time, it would be redeemed or purchased back for a price. The stewardship of Naboth's parcel had probably been in his family for generations. He therefore really could not sell the land, for it belonged not only to him but also to his past and future family.

The possession of such a parcel of land also entailed certain rights and status in society that would have passed to Naboth as a natural inheritance. To give up the land would not only break the link with his forebears but also sever his ties with the society in

which he had been raised. What would he then do? Where would
he go? How would he reestablish himself in a new community?
The ideas of moving one's residence from place to place or changing occupations that are so common in our era would have been
very foreign to the people of his day. In certain areas even today,
you never have a sense of really belonging socially unless you are
born in a town. Even with monetary compensation or another
vineyard in exchange for his, Naboth would have to start over.
Such a prospect may have seemed overwhelming.

It also appears that without some exigent reason of state, the
king of Israel could not unilaterally appropriate privately held
land. With all these reasons in mind, Naboth's response to Ahab's
proposal was simply no. What legal recourse did Ahab have when
confronted with such a refusal? Apparently none. What could he
then do, having been deprived of his desire? Exactly what we
might expect of someone whose character has been so well portrayed in so few words: he pouted and sulked. "And Ahab came
into his house heavy and displeased because of the word which
Naboth the Jezreelite had spoken to him: for he had said, I will not
give thee the inheritance of my fathers. And [Ahab] laid him
down upon his bed, and turned away his face, and would eat no
bread." (1 Kings 21:4.) Ahab's feelings when he returned unsuc-
cessful in obtaining Naboth's vineyard were "heavy and displeased," or, in another translation, "much excited and angry."[1]
The same words describe his reaction in 1 Kings 20:43, upon his
being informed by a prophetic messenger that Ahab's life would be
forfeited because he spared that of Israel's archenemy, Ben-hadad
of Syria. Ahab developed a patterned response to bad news.
Indeed, he had a true attitude problem.

Since he stopped eating, it would have been impossible for his
queen, Jezebel, not to notice his sulking. She approached him and
asked, "Why is thy spirit so sad, that thou eatest no bread?" (1 Kings
21:5.) She was undoubtedly familiar with the pettiness of his feelings, but she apparently did not know what had generated this
bout. We can envision Ahab lying on his bed, facing the wall, responding with a whiny longing in his voice, "Because I spake unto
Naboth the Jezreelite, and said unto him, Give me thy vineyard for

money; or else, if it please thee, I will give thee another vineyard for it: and he answered, I will not give thee my vineyard" (1 Kings 21:6). Jezebel responded, "Dost thou now govern the kingdom of Israel?" (1 Kings 21:7.) This phrase has been understood many ways. Perhaps it expressed defiance: "Who does Naboth think he is to deny the king?" Or perhaps Jezebel was sarcastically chiding her husband for whining over such an insignificant thing. Or maybe the translation of the phrase as "Are you or are you not king in Israel?"[2] indicates neither disdain of Naboth nor sarcasm but merely a question displaying Jezebel's view of what it meant to be king. Her previous imposition of Baal worship and her later actions regarding Naboth certainly certify that her view of kingship tended more toward absolute monarchy than the traditional Israelite idea of the king being the Lord's servant to govern the people.

Jezebel directed her sullen husband, "Arise, and eat bread, and let thine heart be merry: I will give thee the vineyard of Naboth the Jezreelite" (1 Kings 21:7). We may assume that Ahab resumed his kingly posture, but are left to wonder if he ever inquired of Jezebel how she intended to fulfill her promise. This record of a pouting king being advised to be of good cheer by an iniquitous woman reminds us of another such account in Ether 8. There Jared, king of the Jaredites, was introduced to secret combinations by his scheming daughter. Jezebel proceeded to write letters in her husband's name, seal them with his royal seal, and send them "unto the elders and to the nobles that were in his city, dwelling with Naboth" (1 Kings 21:8). It seems probable that the well-being of the city leaders and nobility throughout the kingdom depended principally on the wishes of the king. That would have been especially true of those inhabiting a city where one of the royal palaces resided. Without any indication of questioning the royal wish, the city elders carried out the directives contained in Jezebel's forged letters.

And what were those instructions? "Proclaim a fast, and set Naboth on high among the people: and set two men, sons of Belial, before him, to bear witness against him, saying, Thou didst blaspheme God and the king. And then carry him out, and stone him, that he may die." (1 Kings 21:9–10.) The proclamation of a fast was probably done on the pretext of the need to discover the cause of some local misfortune. In the Old Testament, leaders frequently declared fasts to find the cause of a problem affecting the people or to ward off some impending peril (see Judges 20:20–27; Joel 1:13–15; 2:15–17; Jeremiah 14:1, 12). The meaning of the phrase that Naboth should be set "on high" continues to be a matter of debate. It may signify that he was to be set in front of the people in a high place, as one in the seat of the accused on trial before the elders of the people. Or it could mean that he was to be positioned in a place of honor, so that when the accusation was made against him, it would be even more serious because of his exalted position. This latter approach seems more likely. The "sons of Belial" refers to good-for-nothings or scoundrels, those of low moral character who would perjure themselves for money.

It is interesting that of all the accusations Jezebel might have conjured up to be used against Naboth, she chose blasphemy. Such a charge required no stolen goods or dead body as proof, only the testimony of false witnesses, which could be easily arranged. Ironically, she chose to charge Naboth with the very crime of which she herself was guilty. In a similar way, Laman and Lemuel accused their brother Nephi of the evil designs that were, in reality, their own, not his (see 1 Nephi 16:37–38). There seems to be a human tendency to judge others negatively by seeing in them the evils that lurk in our own hearts. That realization should temper all of us in our inclination to judge, remembering that "with what judgment ye judge, ye shall be judged: and with what measure ye mete, it shall be measured to you again" (Matthew 7:2).

Jezebel's plan unfolded according to her desires. On the pretext that he had cursed God and the king, Naboth was falsely identified as the cause of the people's existing or pending distress. He was condemned and subsequently destroyed. 2 Kings 9:26 indicates that his sons were executed with him in conformity with Israelite practice (see Numbers 16:27, 32–33; Joshua 7:24–25; 2 Samuel 21:6). Society seemed to fear that the sons would perpetuate their father's supposed blasphemy, thus carrying out the curse. According to those laws known as "escheat," which still exist today, if there is no surviving heir to property, it is forfeited to the crown. Jezebel's plan worked flawlessly. Yet this whole evil scenario raises a troubling question. In the midst of an era of growth and expansion, was the taking of Naboth's vineyard an isolated incident or just one of many such acquisitions? We do not know for sure. Either way, this act of immorality stands out for its sheer perfidy.

The queen realized her wish and presented the vineyard to her husband. Thus "it came to pass, when Jezebel heard that Naboth was stoned, and was dead, that Jezebel said to Ahab, Arise, take possession of the vineyard of Naboth the Jezreelite, which he refused to give thee for money: for Naboth is not alive, but dead" (1 Kings 21:15). The scripture gives no clue that Ahab asked how Naboth's death had occurred. He simply seemed pleased to at last get the vineyard. He "rose up to go down to the vineyard of Naboth the Jezreelite, to take possession of it" (1 Kings 21:16). It is instructive to see how easily Ahab and Jezebel ignored those of the ten commandments that relate to our relationship with our fellowmen when they had already broken the first two commandments, which concern our relationship to God. Having disobeyed "Thou shalt have no other gods before me" and "Thou shalt not make unto thee any graven image" (Exodus 20:3–4), it seemed quite natural for them to break the commandments against covetousness, stealing, bearing false witness, and, ultimately, murder. Indeed, they breached all of these within the first 14 verses of chapter 21. According to 2 Chronicles 21:13, they also broke the command to refrain from adultery. This is a powerful lesson to us all and should teach us to remember that if our relationship with God is wrong, nothing else can go right. On the other hand, the lesson from the lives of those who follow the Lord is that if obeying him is our first priority, all else will eventually fall into place.

In some ways, it seems as though this story of taking Naboth's vineyard should end in chapter 21, verse 16. Yet verse 17 is where it really begins. All that precedes seems only to set the stage for the sudden arrival of Elijah. Just as the prophet's initial appearance in Jericho seemed abrupt, Ahab must have felt that Elijah appeared out of nowhere this time. As Ahab happily journeyed to take possession of Naboth's vineyard, "the word of the Lord came to Elijah the Tishbite, saying, Arise, go down to meet Ahab king of Israel, which is in Samaria: behold, he is in the vineyard of Naboth, whither he is gone down to possess it" (1 Kings 21:17–18).

Remember that throughout Ahab's reign, the kingdom of Israel enjoyed relative security and prosperity. Elijah's constant harangues must have discomfited everyone at court. He was continually calling them to accountability. Ahab seemed to be happy only twice in this whole narrative. One of those times occurred when he correctly predicted that Micaiah, another prophet of Jehovah, would prophesy evil against him (see 1 Kings 22:7–18). The other happened when he went to take possession of Naboth's vineyard. The Lord, through his prophets, would not allow Ahab to enjoy happiness in iniquity, "which thing is contrary to the nature of that righteousness which is in our great and Eternal Head" (Helaman 13:38). As Alma so clearly stated, "Behold, I say unto you, wickedness never was happiness" (Alma 41:10). The Lord was not about to let Ahab forget that. Therefore, his message to the king of Israel on this occasion declared, "Thus saith the Lord, Hast thou killed, and also taken possession? . . . In the place where dogs licked the blood of Naboth shall dogs lick thy blood, even thine." (1 Kings 21:19.)

The meeting between the prophet and the king would definitely not be classified as a happy reunion. Ahab, who once accused Elijah of troubling Israel (see 1 Kings 18:17), now addressed him thus: "Hast thou found me, O mine enemy?" Elijah responded, "I have found thee: because thou hast sold thyself to work evil in the sight of the Lord." (1 Kings 21:20.) The Lord made a similar accusation in the Pearl of Great Price, indicating that some of Noah's descendants had "sold themselves" (Moses 8:15). In this context, the phrase means to sell oneself short, to give oneself over to one's lusts, to relinquish one's will to evil and thus to voluntarily enslave oneself. Remember that the Lord executes judgment in righteousness and that "if they are condemned they bring upon themselves their own condemnation" (Helaman 14:29). The consequences of Ahab's selling himself to do evil now brought from Elijah's mouth the Lord's decree.

In essence, Elijah confronted and condemned both monarchs for their evils, even though he did not speak to Jezebel in person.

The judgment he pronounced assured the gruesome deaths of both king and queen. Not only were they to die, but Jezebel and some of their posterity were to suffer the added disgrace of lacking burial. Additionally, and most calamitous of all, their family line would become extinct. "Behold, I will bring evil upon thee, and will take away thy posterity, and will cut off from Ahab him that pisseth against the wall [that is to say, all living descendants], and him that is shut up and left in Israel, and will make thine house like the house of Jeroboam the son of Nebat, and like the house of Baasha the son of Ahijah, for the provocation wherewith thou hast provoked me to anger, and made Israel to sin. And of Jezebel also spake the Lord, saying, The dogs shall eat Jezebel by the wall of Jezreel. Him that dieth of Ahab in the city the dogs shall eat; and him that dieth in the field shall the fowls of the air eat." (1 Kings 21:21–24.) This grim prophecy that Ahab's family would cease to exist, given from the lips of the prophet whose mission pertained to the covenants and ordinances that bind families eternally, causes us to shudder.

As if to remind us of all he had previously written, the author of 1 Kings then reemphasized: "But there was none like unto Ahab, which did sell himself to work wickedness in the sight of the Lord, whom Jezebel his wife stirred up. And he did very abominably in following idols, according to all things as did the Amorites, whom the Lord cast out before the children of Israel." (1 Kings 21:25–26.) This reminder makes Ahab's response to Elijah's pronouncement nothing less than a miracle: "And it came to pass, when Ahab heard those words, that he rent his clothes, and put sackcloth upon his flesh, and fasted, and lay in sackcloth, and went softly" (1 Kings 21:27). Of the many types of miracles, none is more remarkable than the changing of a heart.

Ahab indicated his state of sadness and mourning by rending or ripping his clothes, a traditional sign of grief among the Israelites. He wore sackcloth, a rough burlap-like material that would chafe the skin, as an act of penance. He fasted, presumably for the same reasons we do, to sublimate his natural passions and humbly seek the Lord. He "went softly," or sadly or dejectedly. From all appearances, he experienced the sorrow for sin that we term repentance. Given Ahab's history, it is easy to understand why some have questioned his motives. But the Lord, who "looketh on the heart" (1 Samuel 16:7), confirmed to Elijah that it was not just a matter of appearances: "And the word of the Lord came to Elijah the Tishbite, saying, Seest thou how Ahab humbleth himself before me? because he humbleth himself before me, I will not bring the evil in his days: but in his son's days will I bring the evil upon his house." (1 Kings 21:28–29.) He who alone can judge our hearts decided to postpone the pronounced sentence. After all we have learned about Ahab's character, to see him humble himself before the Lord is to witness the truly miraculous. If Ahab could humble himself sufficiently to obtain a postponement of the pronounced condemnation, will not the Lord also extend mercy to the rest of us if we humble ourselves to "the depths of humility"? (Mosiah 4:11.) Repentance and forgiveness are truly great miracles, and remain available to us only because of the greatest miracle of all, the atonement of Jesus Christ.

We should recognize another important lesson presented here, namely that we are not authorized to pronounce final judgments on anyone, even Ahab. God alone is "the Judge of all the earth" (Genesis 18:25). He has commanded us: "Judge not unrighteously" (JST, Matthew 7:1). Instead, we are to become like him, loving "righteousness and judgment" (Psalm 33:5) and being *merciful*, or full of mercy. He may have "mercy on whom he will have mercy" (Romans 9:18), but of us "it is required to forgive all men" (D&C 64:10). To be worthy to be called his children, we must acquire even those attributes of justice and mercy alluded to by the prophet Micah: "Who is a God like unto thee, that pardoneth iniquity, and passeth by the transgression of the remnant of his heritage? he retaineth not his anger for ever, because he delighteth in mercy." (Micah 7:18.)

Chapter Ten

THE DEATHS OF
AHAB AND AHAZIAH

———

THE LORD POSTPONED BUT DID NOT rescind the prophesied destruction of Ahab's family. It is difficult to gauge exactly how Ahab's penance affected his own demise. His death at the hands of the Syrian army during an attack on Ramoth-Gilead are detailed in the chapter immediately following the one containing Elijah's prophecy. Ahab joined forces with Jehoshaphat, the king of Judah, to battle Syria. Ahab entered the battle in disguise but that was not enough to protect him. "A certain man drew a bow at a venture, and smote the king of Israel between the joints of the harness: wherefore he said unto the driver of his chariot, Turn thine hand, and carry me out of the host; for I am wounded" (1 Kings 22:34). The phrase "between the joints of the harness" refers to the unprotected area between his armor and breastplate, meaning that the arrow pierced him. The narrative continues: "And the battle increased that day: and the king was stayed up in his chariot against the Syrians, and died at even: and the blood ran out of the wound into the midst of the chariot. . . . So the king died, and was brought to Samaria; and they buried the king in Samaria. And one washed the chariot in the pool of Samaria; and the dogs licked up his blood; and they washed his armour; according unto the word of the Lord which he spake." (1 Kings 22:35, 37–38.) Thus ended the reign and the mortal life of Ahab, king of Israel.

Ahab's son, Ahaziah, succeeded him as king and "did evil in the sight of the Lord, and walked in the way of his father, and in the way of his mother" (1 Kings 22:52). About two years into his reign, Ahaziah "fell down through a lattice in his upper chamber that was in Samaria, and was sick." Without more information, it is not possible to reconstruct exactly what accident befell the new king. Houses in the Near East are constructed with flat roofs that serve as either floors for upper stories or porches and patios. It is hard to decipher whether Ahaziah fell through a lattice work on the floor of such an upper story or through some kind of side panel forming a railing. He apparently suffered a major fall and sustained critical injuries. The scripture probably refers to those unhealed injuries when it says he was sick. In this seriously injured state, the king "sent messengers, and said unto them, Go, enquire of Baal-zebub the god of Ekron whether I shall recover of this disease." (2 Kings 1:2.) Ekron, a Philistine city located southwest of Jerusalem, was a considerable distance from Samaria. The king must have been in great distress to send messengers such a distance for a personal psychic reading.

Strong evidence throughout the narrative about Elijah demonstrates that signs and miracles do not convert. For instance, the miracle of the perpetuation of the meal and oil was not enough to shore up the widow of Zarephath's faith against the loss of her son. Although Obadiah, Ahab's servant, had undoubtedly been blessed by the Lord for hiding the prophets from Jezebel's wrath, he sought further assurances before willfully heeding Elijah's command to announce his arrival to Ahab. Ahab seemed to miss the repeated miraculous messages to repent, or, at least, they never seemed to sink in until near the end of his life when, under penalty of death, he finally began to understand. After all that had happened to his father, Ahab, Ahaziah still sent to Baal-zebub for a sign. Perhaps that very callousness and hard-heartedness also brought upon him the severity of his condemnation. Whereas "signs follow those that believe" because they are the natural result of faith, the Lord warns us against seeking signs, for "he that seeketh signs shall see signs, but not unto salvation" (D&C 63:9, 7). Ahab's idolatrous family members sought signs and received them, but "only in wrath unto their condemnation" (D&C 63:11).

So, Ahaziah proceeded to seek a sign from Baal-zebub. The name Baal-zebub literally means "the Lord of the flies." Perhaps the name of this Philistine deity referred to the god's supposed power to control weather, of which flies are monitors or harbingers. Or, perhaps the involvement of flies in cases of sickness and death implied that this god had some jurisdiction over them. Or it may be that the original name of the deity was Baal Zebul (Baal is prince), which Hebrew scribes later altered to read Baal-zebub as an insult. It is hard to tell. Regardless of the background of the Philistine idol's name, why did Ahaziah send to Ekron at all? Why not contact the local Baal priests in Samaria? Perhaps he feared divulging the seriousness of his injury to the locals because of intrigues within the government. Or maybe he believed the "grass to be greener on the other side," especially if the Philistine god had a better reputation for healing. It would not be surprising to learn that the Baal of Samaria had proved a poor support to Ahaziah's previous needs. It may also be that the Philistine Baal of Ekron had a reputation for divination (see 1 Samuel 6:2; Isaiah 2:6). The brevity of the scriptural text precludes our having answers to these questions.

Whatever the king's specific reasoning, the messengers departed. As they left on their journey, "the angel of the Lord said to Elijah the Tishbite, Arise, go up to meet the messengers of the king of Samaria, and say unto them, Is it not because there is not a God in Israel, that ye go to enquire of Baal-zebub, the god of Ekron? Now therefore thus saith the Lord, Thou shalt not come down from that bed on which thou art gone up, but shalt surely die" (2 Kings 1:3–4). The true God, Jehovah, would answer Ahaziah's question even though the king had not addressed it to him. "Elijah departed" (2 Kings 1:4), apparently encountered the king's emissaries, and delivered to them the message from the Lord. They then returned to the king, who asked them, "Why are ye now turned back?" (2 Kings 1:5.) At that point, the king's messengers became the Lord's messengers, delivering to the king the message communicated to them by Elijah.

Evidently, Elijah had not introduced himself to the messengers, since Ahaziah inquired of them, "What manner of man was he which came up to meet you, and told you these words?" (2 Kings 1:7.) They responded, "He was an hairy man, and girt with a girdle of leather about his loins" (2 Kings 1:8). The reference to "hairy" could mean that Elijah wore long hair and a full beard or, more likely, refers to his wearing a garment of animal skins covered with hair or wool on the outside. Most individuals in society would have worn clothing made from woven materials instead. It appears that the mantle of the prophet was easily recognizable as something relatively unique because of the way the messengers mentioned it. Their description parallels that given of John the Baptist, who "was clothed with camel's hair, and a with a girdle of a skin about his loins" (Mark 1:6). The description, though seemingly brief and vague, was sufficient to be immediately recognized by King Ahaziah: "It is Elijah the Tishbite" (2 Kings 1:8).

The king then sent "a captain of fifty with his fifty" to Elijah. Ahaziah's intent in doing so can only have been hostile, to either capture or kill the prophet. Elijah's location must have been known to the captain and his company, either because the general area of his habitation was a matter of common knowledge or because Elijah's meeting with the king's messengers pinpointed it. The captain "went up to him: and, behold, he sat on the top of an hill. And he spake unto him, Thou man of God, the king hath said, Come down." (2 Kings 1:9.) Apparently without moving from the spot where he sat, Elijah responded, "If I be a man of God, then let fire come down from heaven, and consume thee and thy fifty." The account continues, "And there came down fire from heaven, and consumed him and his fifty." (2 Kings 1:10.)

Ahaziah either received word from someone of what had happened or surmised that something had gone awry when the captain and fifty did not return. He "sent unto him another captain of fifty with his fifty. And he answered and said unto him, O man of God, thus hath the king said, Come down quickly." (2 Kings 1:11.) This second captain, more demanding and more insistent than the first, commanded Elijah to come down "quickly" or "at once."[1] Elijah's response was the same as that given to the previous request: "If I be a man of God, let fire come down from heaven, and consume thee and thy fifty." The result was also the same: "And the fire of God came down from heaven, and consumed him and his fifty." (2 Kings 1:12.) There is a play on words here in the Hebrew. Elijah essentially said, "If I am a man of God"—*isch Elohim*—"let the fire of God"—*esch Elohim*—"come down from heaven."

The news of the destruction of the first two groups had now reached the king, but he sent a third group of fifty anyway. While Ahaziah may not have understood the message, the captain of the third group of fifty surely had. "And the third captain of fifty went up, and came and fell on his knees before Elijah, and besought him, and said unto him, O man of God, I pray thee, let my life, and the life of these fifty thy servants, be precious in thy sight. Behold, there came fire down from heaven, and burnt up the two captains of the former fifties with their fifties: therefore let my life now be precious in thy sight." (2 Kings 1:13–14.) The attitude of the third captain was totally different from that of the first two. Rather than demanding that Elijah accompany him, he approached Elijah on his knees and pleaded for his life and the lives of his followers, calling them the prophet's "servants." This marked change of demeanor probably would have evoked mercy and forbearance from Elijah under any circumstances, but we shall never know what the prophet's response might otherwise have been, because an angel intervened at that moment. He instructed Elijah, "Go down with him: be not afraid of him." Elijah then "arose, and went down with him unto the king." (2 Kings 1:15.)

Note that Elijah made no move at all to comply with the king's command to come down the first, second, or even third time. The command of the mortal ruler of Israel had no visible effect on him. Conversely, the command of Israel's Heavenly King warranted Elijah's immediate and total submission. While seemingly immune to human pressure, he remained absolutely subservient to the divine will communicated to him by the angel. At his meeting with the king, Elijah did no more than repeat the divine message that had already been communicated to the ruler. "Thus saith the Lord, . . . thou shalt not come down off that bed on which thou art gone up, but shalt surely die" (2 Kings 1:16).

The text records no verbal response by Ahaziah to the Lord's prophecy through Elijah. He just died.

Some readers have been extremely disturbed by Elijah's actions in calling down fire from heaven to destroy the two groups of fifty sent by Ahaziah. They interpret these actions to be unfair, or a misuse of power, or a tarnishing of his prophetic image. Others see them as acceptable only because of the Old Testament mentality of "an eye for an eye." Christian commentators have tended to view the Lord's rebuke of his Apostles James and John recorded in Luke 9 as a condemnation of Elijah, an indication that under the new law established by Christ, Elijah's actions could not be condoned.[2] But is such an interpretation of this experience accurate?

The interaction between the Lord and his two Apostles recounted in Luke 9 followed an incident which occurred while they traveled through Samaria. The Lord was on his way to Jerusalem and "sent messengers before his face: and they went, and entered into a village of the Samaritans, to make ready for him. And they did not receive him, because his face was as though he would go to Jerusalem." (Luke 9:52–53.) Apparently, the Samaritans refused to receive and assist the Lord because he was headed to Jerusalem and the Samaritans and Jews were not on good terms. When James and John saw this rudeness, they said, "Lord, wilt thou that we command fire to come down from heaven, and consume them, even as Elias did?" (Luke 9:54.) Elias is the translation from the Greek for the Hebrew name Elijah. The Lord responded with a rebuke, "Ye know not what manner of spirit ye are of. For the Son of man is not come to destroy men's lives, but to save them." (Luke 9:55–56.)

It appears James and John responded inappropriately to the lack of hospitality by the Samaritans. They simply overreacted, for there is no evidence they made the proposal because their lives were threatened as Elijah's had been. The Lord's response indicates that the brothers were not acting out of a sense of zeal to defend the Lord's words or work, nor out of a need for self-defense. Their emotions or reasoning must have been negatively motivated, perhaps by embarrassment or anger. Thus, the Lord's comment to them did not condemn Elijah, but rather rebuked the attitude then animating the "sons of thunder" (Mark 3:17).

Elijah's case was clearly different. The original messengers of Ahaziah, those sent to Ekron, and the last, the third group of fifty, were submissive to Elijah's authority over that of the king. They essentially abandoned their royal commission and obeyed Elijah. To the contrary, the first and second groups of fifty sought to impose the will of the king over that of the "man of God." By threatening the life of the prophet, they sought to thwart the purposes of the Lord. The Lord himself informed Nephi that he "slayeth the wicked to bring forth his righteous purposes. It is better that one man should perish than that a nation should dwindle and perish in unbelief." (1 Nephi 4:13.) In Nephi's case, it was one man; in Elijah's, it was one hundred.

But was it really the Lord's will that they be destroyed? Apparently, yes. The servant does not superimpose his will over that of the Master. The Lord obviously approved of Elijah's actions, for the Lord sent the fire from heaven. Elijah was a prophet, not a magician. He alone could not make the fire descend; only the Lord could do that. It is also possible that Elijah's words to the two sets of soldiers were not a command for fire to come at all but rather a prophecy of what was about to happen. Throughout Elijah's life, he received great power because of his submission to the Lord's will. Compare the raising of the son of the widow of Zarephath to the demise of Ahaziah. As the Lord's messenger, Elijah had power to speak the words of life or death. It is likely that the Lord at some point had said to him as he did later to Nephi, the son of Helaman, "Behold, I will bless thee forever; and I will make thee mighty in word and in deed, in faith and in works; yea, even that all things shall be done unto thee according to thy word, for thou shalt not ask that which is contrary to my will" (Helaman 10:5).

Chapter Eleven

THE DESTRUCTION OF AHAB'S FAMILY

THUS, IN FULFILLMENT OF THE PROPHECY of Elijah, both Ahab and his son Ahaziah died. But what of the rest of the family? Ahaziah's brother Jehoram (or Joram) began to reign over Israel in his stead. Of him, the record states, "He wrought evil in the sight of the Lord; but not like his father, and like his mother: for he put away the image of Baal that his father had made. Nevertheless he cleaved unto the sins of Jeroboam the son of Nebat, which made Israel to sin; he departed not therefrom." (2 Kings 3:2–3.)

At about the same time, another Jehoram, the firstborn son of righteous King Jehoshaphat, began to reign in Judah. He took to wife the daughter of Ahab, named Athaliah, and "walked in the way of the kings of Israel, as did the house of Ahab . . . : and he did evil in the sight of the Lord" (2 Kings 8:18). Perhaps because of the influence of his wife or because of his own natural inclinations, Jehoram tried to impose the idolatry of the kingdom of Israel on the inhabitants of Judah. "Moreover he made high places in the mountains of Judah, and caused the inhabitants of Jerusalem to commit fornication, and compelled Judah thereto" (2 Chronicles 21:11).

As a result of this wickedness, Elijah sent him a "writing." We have no other reference to Elijah's being involved with the kingdom of Judah except for his earlier trip through Beersheba, the southern-most city of Judah, on his way to Horeb. Elijah's written words to the king mirror the directness and power of his spoken ones:

> Thus saith the Lord God of David thy father, Because thou hast not walked in the ways of Jehoshaphat thy father, nor in the ways of Asa king of Judah,
>
> But hast walked in the way of the kings of Israel, and hast made Judah and the inhabitants of Jerusalem to go a whoring, like to the whoredoms of the house of Ahab, and also hast slain thy brethren of thy father's house, which were better than thyself:
>
> Behold, with a great plague will the Lord smite thy people, and thy children, and thy wives, and all thy goods:
>
> And thou shalt have great sickness by disease of thy bowels, until thy bowels fall out by reason of the sickness day by day. (2 Chronicles 21:12–15.)

This gruesome prophecy was completely fulfilled. Speaking of Jehoram, the author of 2 Chronicles says simply that he "departed without being desired" (21:20).

Following Jehoram of Judah's ignominious death, his son, Ahaziah (or Azariah), who would have been Ahab's grandson, ascended to the throne. Like his father, this new king "walked in the way of the house of Ahab, and did evil in the sight of the Lord" (2 Kings 8:27). The intermarriage of his father, Jehoram, king of Judah, with the family of Ahab of Israel led to political and military alliances between the two kingdoms. That relationship also caused the evils of false worship to infect and spread throughout the southern kingdom.

During the time spanning all these dynastic changes in the two kingdoms, Elijah's successor, Elisha, arranged to carry out the Lord's directive that Jehu be anointed king of Israel. Elisha sent one of his faithful followers to Jehu, who then served as a captain in the army of Israel. Jehu was anointed with oil and had the following blessing pronounced upon him: "Thus saith the Lord God of Israel, I have anointed thee king over the people of the Lord, even over Israel. And thou shalt smite the house of Ahab thy master, that I may avenge the blood of my servants the prophets, and the blood of all the servants of the Lord, at the hand of Jezebel. For the whole house of Ahab shall perish." (2 Kings 9:6–8.) Jehu took this charge seriously and proceeded quickly to accomplish it. He drove his chariot "furiously" (v. 20) toward Jezreel, where Ahab's son Jehoram, king of Israel, was recovering from wounds received in a battle with Syria.

It so happened that Ahaziah, king of Judah, was then visiting his uncle Jehoram, king of Israel, at the latter's palace in Jezreel. Upon word of Jehu's approach, both kings went forth to meet him. Jehoram asked, "Is it peace, Jehu?" to which the newly anointed and commissioned captain replied tersely, "What peace, so long as the whoredoms of thy mother Jezebel and her witchcrafts are so many?" (2 Kings 9:22.) As the full realization of the threat struck Jehoram, he turned to flee, yelling to his nephew, "There is treachery, O Ahaziah" (v. 23). The account continues: "And Jehu drew a bow with his full strength, and smote Jehoram between his arms, and the arrow went out at his heart, and he sunk down in his chariot" (v. 24). Jehu commanded that Jehoram's body be cast into the very field that had once belonged to Naboth, "according to the word of the Lord" (v. 26). Ahaziah fled, but not fast enough. Jehu's men caught him, smote him, and the wounded king of Judah fled across the plains of Esdraelon, only to die in the fortress city of Megiddo.

Having dispatched the kings of both Israel and Judah, Jehu continued his journey to Jezreel. At his approach, the queen mother, Jezebel, "painted her face, and tired her head" (2 Kings 9:30). "Tired her head" means she adorned or fixed her hair. She had previously lost her husband, Ahab, and now, in one moment, she lost her son and grandson. Yet, for one such as Jezebel, vanity continued even in the face of calamity. Dressed in all her finery, she looked out her window, which must have been over the wall of the city, and made a sarcastic remark to Jehu concerning an earlier king of Israel who reigned only seven days after slaying his predecessor: "Had Zimri peace, who slew his master?" (v. 31.) Her biting tongue invited her fate. The scriptural record tells it clearly:

And [Jehu] lifted up his face to the window, and said, Who is on my side? who? And there looked out to him two or three eunuchs.

And he said, Throw her down. So they threw her down: and some of her blood was sprinkled on the wall, and on the horses: and he trode her under foot.

And when he was come in, he did eat and drink, and said, Go, see now this cursed woman, and bury her: for she is a king's daughter.

And they went to bury her: but they found no more of her than the skull, and the feet, and the palms of her hands.

Wherefore they came again, and told him. And he said, This is the word of the Lord, which he spake by his servant Elijah the Tishbite, saying, In the portion of Jezreel shall dogs eat the flesh of Jezebel. (Vv. 32–36.)

In one day, Ahab's wife, son, and grandson died. But more was yet to come. Jehu took charge and commanded in writing that the leaders of the people send forth the best of Ahab's remaining sons to contend with him. The kings of Israel and Judah practiced plural marriage, so Ahab had many sons. Nevertheless, the people feared Jehu, saying, "Behold, two kings stood not before him: how then shall we stand?" (2 Kings 10:4.) The frightened leaders therefore gathered together seventy of the sons of Ahab, beheaded them, and sent their heads to Jehu. Jehu deposited the heads overnight in two piles near the gate of the city. The following morning "he went out, and stood, and said to all the people, Ye be righteous: behold, I conspired against my master, and slew him: but who slew all these? Know now that there shall fall unto the earth nothing of the word of the Lord, which the Lord spake concerning the house of Ahab: for the Lord hath done that which he spake by his servant Elijah. So Jehu slew all that remained of the house of Ahab in Jezreel, and all his great men, and his kinsfolks, and his priests, until he left him none remaining." (Vv. 9–11.)

Meanwhile, in Judah, Athaliah, daughter of Ahab and widow of Jehoram (who died when his bowels fell out), learned that her son Ahaziah had been slain. She proceeded to take control of the kingdom by ordering the death of "all the seed royal" (2 Kings 11:1), which included her own descendants. One of them was spared, however; a young son of Ahaziah was hidden by his nurse.

Eventually, this sole survivor, Joash (or Jehoash), regained the throne and slew Athaliah (see v. 16). Under the tutelage of a priest faithful to Jehovah, this new king repudiated the false worship of his ancestors, Ahaziah, Jehoram and Athaliah, and Ahab and Jezebel. It is recorded of him that he "did that which was right in the sight of the Lord all his days" (2 Kings 12:2). Thus, again, the Lord's promises were fulfilled. Not only did he destroy the wicked members of the family of Ahab as prophesied, but he forgave and favored the descendant who returned to him, in accordance with his promise that the house of David, of which Joash was also a part, would not be destroyed.

From a broader perspective, the Lord treated the extended family of Ahab according to general principles he had established centuries earlier for his relationship to his chosen people: "Thou shalt not bow down thyself unto them [false gods or graven images], nor serve them: for I the Lord thy God am a jealous God, visiting the iniquity of the fathers upon the children unto the third and fourth generation of them that hate me, and shewing mercy unto thousands of them that love me and keep my commandments" (Deuteronomy 5:9–10). Clearly, those thousands whom he loves include those children of the wicked "who repent, or the children's children, [who] turn to the Lord their God, with all their hearts and with all their might, mind, and strength" (D&C 98:47). The recitation of Elijah's prophecies to Ahab and their resultant fulfillment are but one of many examples witnessing that the holy scriptures *are* a record of the verification of the Lord's promises; for he truly fulfills all his words.

Chapter Twelve

THE
DEPARTURE

JUST AS THE LORD FULFILLS HIS PROMISES, he also verifies the words and works of his prophets. For this reason, he arranged to put a stamp of approval on Elijah's life and mission by orchestrating the prophet's miraculous departure from the earth. Once Elijah had completed all that the Lord assigned him to accomplish, his mortal mission quickly drew to a close. That being the case, he journeyed to the pre-appointed place for his departure.

"And it came to pass, when the Lord would take up Elijah into heaven by a whirlwind, that Elijah went with Elisha from Gilgal" (2 Kings 2:1). The Gilgal mentioned here may not be the same city commonly referred to in the Old Testament, which city lay near Jericho and was the site where Joshua set up camp after crossing the Jordan to enter the land of Canaan (see Joshua 4:19; 5:10). If it was that location, Elijah and Elisha traveled westward from the Jordan valley up into the hills to Bethel and then returned to the valley whence they started. The route seems circuitous unless Elijah received some vital aspect of preparation in Bethel. After all, he did indicate that the Lord specifically "sent" him to Bethel (2 Kings 2:2). Or, it may be that the Gilgal referred to is the one mentioned in Deuteronomy 11:30, which would have been farther to the northwest in the hill country of Samaria. This would suggest that Elijah and Elisha started from the center of the northern kingdom on their route toward the river Jordan, thus arriving at Bethel and Jericho as natural stops along the route. Since the scripture does say they went "down" to Bethel (2 Kings 2:2) and that term in the Hebrew text usually denotes a descent in elevation, either they ascended from the Jordan valley to a point in elevation higher than Bethel and then descended to it, or they went there from another, more obscure location named Gilgal that was situated at a higher level, perhaps the one referenced in Deuteronomy.

Bethel, meaning literally the "house of God," was a sacred site where both Abraham and Jacob communed with the Almighty (see Genesis 12:8; 13:3; 28:19). For some unrecorded reason, Elijah needed to make a final pilgrimage there before his mortal mission was complete. He apparently knew of his coming departure and seems to have wanted Elisha to leave him so he might be alone. "And Elijah said unto Elisha, Tarry here, I pray thee; for the Lord hath sent me to Beth-el." But his follower responded, "As the Lord liveth, and as thy soul liveth, I will not leave thee." (2 Kings 2:2.) Elisha employed a solemn oath invoking the life of God and also, interestingly, the life of Elijah. Usually, when we see such oaths, they are made by the life of God and the life of the speaker. Here, Elisha swore by Elijah's life instead of his own.

When the two arrived at Bethel, "the sons of the prophets that were at Beth-el came forth to Elisha, and said unto him, Knowest thou that the Lord will take away thy master from thy head to day? And he said, Yea, I know it; hold ye your peace." (2 Kings 2:3.) The phrase "sons of the prophets," which appears frequently in chapter 2 of 2 Kings, probably refers to followers of Jehovah who obeyed the prophetic message. The fact that they knew so much about Elijah, his apprentice Elisha, and what was about to happen indicates that they received inspiration and also that Elijah may have pursued a ministry among them about which nothing is recorded. Elisha's response to these followers of the prophets shows that he had at least the general idea of Elijah's imminent departure. Whereas Elijah knew he was about to leave the earth, perhaps he did not realize that Elisha knew it also. Maybe Elisha received independent inspiration about his master's leaving, which gave impetus to his insistence on being with him when the moment arrived.

At Bethel, the same interchange again occurred between Elijah and Elisha. Elijah asked his follower to tarry and Elisha responded with an oath that he would not. After descending the hills to Jericho, which lies in the low-lying Jordan valley, Elisha again met the "sons of the prophets," who asked him if he knew that he was about to lose his master. To them, he also answered, "Yea, I know it; hold ye your peace." (2 Kings 2:5.) Upon leaving Jericho, Elijah asked Elisha a third time to remain behind. For the third time, Elisha refused. So "they two went on" (v. 6). Fifty men of the sons of the prophets followed them as far as the Jordan River (see v. 7).

Standing on the west bank of the Jordan, "Elijah took his mantle, and wrapped it together, and smote the waters, and they were divided hither and thither, so that they two went over on dry ground" (2 Kings 2:8). The mantle of Elijah, with all its symbolic meaning, was used as the instrument to perform this great miracle. Parting the waters and crossing on dry ground obviously evokes memories of Moses' parting the Red Sea (see Exodus 14:13–22), but it also reminds us of Joshua's parting the Jordan when the army of Israel first entered Canaan (see Joshua 3:7–17). Even as Israel crossed westward on dry ground to inherit the promised land, Elijah now crossed eastward to receive the promise of his God.

Speaking of the promised land, the Old Testament prophet Obadiah referred to Gilead and Zarephath as its boundaries (see Obadiah 1:17–21). When first introducing Elijah, the scripture tells us that he was of the inhabitants of Gilead (see 1 Kings 17:1). His travels had taken him from the brook Cherith in Gilead, in the eastern borders of the land, to Zarephath, in the territory of Sidon far to the north, where he was given food and shelter by the widow. He then probably wandered along the western reaches of the promised land from Mount Carmel to Beersheba in the south, then on to Mount Horeb. His return from Mount Horeb brought him up the eastern borders of Judah and Israel toward Syria. His ultimate departure to heaven occurred to the east of the Jordan

River, roughly the same location as that of the translation of Moses. Elijah's journeys seem to have circumscribed the boundaries of the promised land. It was as though his very life drew a circle around the area principally occupied by those who had a peculiar covenant relationship with Jehovah, those who needed to turn their hearts again to the covenant. As Moses had gathered the people, brought them to know God, and delivered them to this spot east of Jordan, Elijah had now drawn a circle around that same covenant people and come to this place to return them to their God.

"And it came to pass, when they were gone over, that Elijah said unto Elisha, Ask what I shall do for thee, before I be taken away from thee. And Elisha said, I pray thee, let a double portion of thy spirit be upon me." (2 Kings 2:9.) Elijah responded, "Thou hast asked a hard thing: nevertheless, if thou see me when I am taken from thee, it shall be so unto thee; but if not, it shall not be so" (v. 10). Elisha must have been a faithful and obedient follower. Nonetheless, the magnitude of the request made it something that even Elijah could not bestow. The power to grant such a petition belonged to the Lord alone. If Elisha had the spiritual vision to view Elijah's departure, it would demonstrate that he could penetrate the celestial sphere and envision heavenly things. Thus, he would have the power he requested.

At first reading, Elisha's request seems extraordinary. Was he asking to be better and more powerful than his teacher? No, it appears he simply sought "earnestly the best gifts" (D&C 46:8). By asking for a double portion of Elijah's spirit, Elisha requested to be given the status of a firstborn son, who, under the law of Moses, received a double share of his father's inheritance (see Deuteronomy 12:17). Elisha's reference to Elijah as "my father" (2 Kings 2:12) indicates his great respect for his guide and his sense of dependence upon Elijah, much like a child upon a father. In a sense, as Elisha's teacher, leader, and prophetic master, Elijah became Elisha's spiritual father. Elisha thus requested his perceived birthright, asking that he be established as the true successor of Elijah. Perhaps he also pleaded for powers far beyond his own, to truly be endowed with the power of his predecessor.

They continued their discussion as they walked. But suddenly they were interrupted and separated by a most singular event. "And it came to pass, as they still went on, and talked, that, behold, there appeared a chariot of fire, and horses of fire, and parted them both asunder; and Elijah went up by a whirlwind into heaven" (2 Kings 2:11). A chariot and horses of fire made an instant appearance and a dramatic departure. Since there is no indication of anything actually being burned, the use of the word *fire* here is probably a reference to the appearance of heavenly glory. The scriptures often refer to the manifestation of glory as fire. Glory is difficult to describe, but seems to have some relationship to physical presence, something akin to pure, divine energy accompanied by light. Contrary to the popular conception of *hell* as being a place of fire, Isaiah explained that *heaven* is such a place by asking, "Who among us shall dwell with the devouring fire . . . with everlasting burnings?" The answer? "He that walketh righteously." (Isaiah 33:14–15.) Joseph Smith confirmed that "God Almighty Himself dwells in eternal fire."[1] "And Elisha saw it, and he cried, My father, my father, the chariot of Israel, and the horsemen thereof" (2 Kings 2:12). Elisha's request was granted, for he had seen his companion depart. Note that Elisha's exclamation refers to "horsemen" as well as the horses and chariot. These horsemen were probably angelic escorts for Elijah. When Joseph Smith said, "Spirits can only be revealed in flaming fire and glory,"[2] he was likely alluding to just such appearances as that witnessed by Elisha. The record continues, "And he saw him no more." Finding himself alone, bereaved of his great mentor, the faithful Elisha "took hold of his own clothes, and rent them in two pieces." (2 Kings 2:12.) In symbolic fashion, Elisha indicated his profound grief. As so often happens, even though we anticipate a separation, when the actual moment arrives, we seem to be caught completely unprepared and a wave of sadness overwhelms us.

Just as Elijah had left his pupil a spiritual legacy, he also left him a physical symbol of his power. As Elijah rose upward with his heavenly escort, his mantle had fallen to the earth. Elisha reverently gathered up this token of spiritual birthright and "went back, and stood by the bank of Jordan; and he took the mantle of Elijah that fell from him, and smote the waters, and said, Where is the Lord God of Elijah? and when he also had smitten the waters, they parted hither and thither: and Elisha went over" (2 Kings 2:13–14). At times, the Lord grants his prophets a physical object on which to focus their spiritual energy and faith. Lehi received the Liahona, Joseph Smith the Urim and Thummim, and Elisha the mantle of the prophet. With this passing of the mantle, Elisha assumed the role of prophet. "And when the sons of the prophets which were to view at Jericho saw him, they said, The spirit of Elijah doth rest on Elisha" (2 Kings 2:15). This is the only place in our standard works where the precise phrase "the spirit of Elijah" appears. It was apparent to those waiting for the prophet's return that the mantle had passed to, or that the power of their great prophetic leader had been conferred upon, another. After the account of a futile three-day search by some of his followers (see 2 Kings 2:16–18), the historical references to Elijah in the Old Testament record cease.

Chapter Thirteen

THE DOCTRINE OF TRANSLATION

WHAT BECAME OF ELIJAH AT THIS POINT? It is interesting here to reflect on the difference between having our own way and doing things the Lord's way. When Elijah became depressed during his journey to Horeb, he told the Lord he had had enough and was ready to die. But to die then, according to Elijah's desire, would have been premature according to the Lord's plan. By deferring instead to the Lord's will, Elijah went on to his climactic visit with Jehovah at Horeb and then to the fulfillment of other important assignments. When the moment actually came in the Lord's time-table for Elijah to leave the earth, he departed in a blaze of glory, a far cry from the lonely death in the desert that he had earlier wished for himself. Elijah had trusted the One who knows "the end from the beginning" (Abraham 2:8) to grant him the proper "end."

But was it "the end"? Where had Elijah gone? Why had the Lord orchestrated this miraculous departure? We refer to Elijah's being taken to heaven without tasting death as "translation." Translation is a change in physical condition that allows one to remain active on the earth in a body of flesh and bone while simultaneously not being subject to the powers of the earth. It is intended to continue for an extended duration. A similar state lasting for a brief period of time is referred to in the scriptures as "transfiguration." Moses said of just such a short-term experience: "But now mine own eyes have beheld God; but not my natural, but my spiritual eyes, for my natural eyes could not have beheld; for I should have withered and died in his presence; but his glory was upon me; and I beheld his face, for I was transfigured before him" (Moses 1:11).

The scriptural references to translation refer to persons being left in that state until their time of resurrection (see D&C 133: 53–55). While inquiring of the Lord about the condition of the Three Nephites, who were in a translated state similar to that of Elijah, the prophet Mormon learned that in order for them not to taste of death, "there was a change wrought upon their bodies, that they might not suffer pain nor sorrow save it were for the sins of the world. Now this change was not equal to that which shall take place at the last day; but there was a change wrought upon them, insomuch that Satan could have no power over them, that he could not tempt them; and they were sanctified in the flesh, that they were holy, and that the powers of the earth could not hold them." (3 Nephi 28:38–39.) Joseph Smith added, "This distinction is made between the doctrine of the actual resurrection and translation: translation obtains deliverance from the tortures and sufferings of the body, but their existence will prolong as to the labors and toils of the ministry, before they can enter into so great a rest and glory."[1] Thus, he observed on another occasion, "translated bodies cannot enter into rest until they have undergone a change equivalent to death. Translated bodies are designed for future missions."[2] Joseph Smith also stated: "Many have supposed that the doctrine of translation was a doctrine whereby men were taken immediately into the presence of God, and into an eternal fullness, but this is a mistaken idea. Their place of habitation is that of the terrestrial order, and a place prepared for such characters He held in reserve to be ministering angels unto many planets, and who as yet have not entered into so great a fullness as those who are resurrected from the dead."[3]

Why would the Lord translate Elijah instead of letting the prophet minister in the spirit world? Simply because the gospel was not preached to the spirits in the spirit world before the visit of Christ there between his crucifixion and resurrection. The Lord's visit there turned the key for the beginning of that work. We learn from the Doctrine and Covenants that from among the righteous in the spirit world the Lord "organized his forces and appointed messengers, clothed with power and authority, and commissioned them to go forth and carry the light of the gospel to them that were in darkness, even to all the spirits of men; and thus was the gospel preached to the dead" (D&C 138:30). This means that if we have been faithful, when we die we continue our labors "in the preaching of the gospel of repentance and redemption, through the sacrifice of the Only Begotten Son of God, among those who are in darkness and under the bondage of sin in the great world of the spirits of the dead" (D&C 138:57). But had Elijah died, he would have been unable to preach to the spirits in prison because that labor had not yet begun.

Likewise, had Elijah died, he would have had to wait for the renewal of his tangible, physical body until after the Lord's resurrection. Since Christ was the first to be resurrected, those who died before his time were unable to come forth to perform any labors requiring such a body. Yet, the Lord needed Elijah to continue in the flesh because of the nature of his future mission. Translation provided a means whereby the prophet could retain his physical body and still continue in the ministry. It seems clear, then, that Elijah's being translated did not end his prophetic assignments, but rather preserved him to fulfill a future mission. And what was that to be? The only Old Testament references to Elijah after his miraculous departure are the final recorded words of the prophet Malachi, which tell us, at least in part, why the Lord carried the prophet to heaven in a chariot of fire. "Behold, I will send you Elijah the prophet before the coming of the great and dreadful day of the Lord: and he shall turn the heart of the fathers to the children, and the heart of the children to their fathers, lest I come and smite the earth with a curse" (Malachi 4:5–6). Those two brief verses opened the gate to a veritable flood of speculations and traditions about the return of Elijah.

Chapter Fourteen

ELIJAH IN THE
NEW TESTAMENT

WITH THE CLOSING VERSES OF THE OLD Testament predicting
the return of Elijah, it is not surprising that the New Testament
record contains questions about his return. Indeed, it stands to reason that Elijah's miraculous departure combined with Malachi's
prophecy would stimulate lively conjecture and expectations
among the remnant of Israel that inhabited the land of Judea at
the time the New Testament record began. Unfortunately, we have
only two records that reveal Judaism's pre-Christian-era expectations regarding Elijah's return in the "last times": the writings of
Malachi and those of a second-century B.C. Jewish scribe named Ben
Sirach. The latter's apocryphal work contains the following lines:

> Till like a fire there appeared the prophet
>> Whose words were as a flaming furnace.
> Their staff of bread he shattered,
>> in his zeal he reduced them to straits;
> By God's word he shut up the heavens
>> and three times brought down fire.
> How awesome are you, Elijah!
>> Whose glory is equal to yours?

You brought a dead man back to life
    from the nether world, by the will of the Lord.
You sent kings down to destruction,
    and nobles, from their beds of sickness.
You heard threats at Sinai,
    at Horeb avenging judgments.
You anointed kings who should inflict vengeance,
    and a prophet as your successor.
You were taken aloft in a whirlwind,
    in a chariot with fiery horses.
You are destined, it is written, in time to come
    to put an end to wrath before the day of the Lord,
To turn back the hearts of fathers toward their sons,
    and to re-establish the tribes of Jacob.
Blessed is he who shall have seen you before he dies,
    O Elijah, enveloped in the whirlwind![1]

This indicates a Jewish anticipation that Elijah would come to deflect the Lord's wrath from the house of Israel, presumably by turning the hearts of the people toward righteousness. Some scholars surmise that there is at least indirect evidence of a rabbinic tradition dating from the reign of Herod the Great that Elijah would come to correct injustice.[2] But the best verification of the existence of such an expectation among the Jews comes from the New Testament Gospels themselves. They confirm that the common people knew of such a tradition and anticipated its fulfillment. It is evident from the questions and comments recorded by the four Gospel authors that the people wondered whether either John the Baptist or Jesus had come in fulfillment of Malachi's promise about Elijah's return.

One of the major confusions affecting our understanding of the New Testament references to Elijah is in the rendition of Elijah's name in Greek as "Elias." Whereas the Old Testament was translated from Hebrew documents, the New Testament was translated from Greek ones. "Elijah" in Hebrew becomes "Elias" in Greek. For most people, that poses no special problem, since they simply assume all such references are to Elijah. But for the Latter-day Saints, it does pose some confusion. We know that in addition to the person named Elijah, whose ministry we are discussing in this volume, there lived another Old Testament personage actually named Elias. The specific identification of this Elias is difficult. We do know he is the person who, along with Moses and Elijah, appeared in the Kirtland Temple in 1836. This clearly distinguishes him from either of them. As recorded by Joseph Smith, Elias "committed the dispensation of the gospel of Abraham, saying that in us and our seed all generations after us should be blessed" (D&C 110:12). This bestowal of the blessings of the Lord's covenant with Abraham upon Joseph Smith and Oliver Cowdery would likely have been done by a person from Abraham's time. Beyond that supposition, we cannot pinpoint exactly who Elias was.

In addition to the need to differentiate between the actual person Elias and the person Elijah in the New Testament, another complicating factor is the gospel-related usage of the term "Elias." In that context, any person sent as a forerunner to build the Lord's kingdom or to prepare the Lord's way or to restore something (see JST, Matthew 17:13–14) may be termed an "Elias." Accordingly, Joseph Smith explained: "The spirit of Elias is to prepare the way for a greater revelation of God, which is the Priesthood of Elias, or the Priesthood that Aaron was ordained unto. And when God sends a man into the world to prepare for a greater work, holding the keys of the power of Elias, it was called the doctrine of Elias, even from the early ages of the world. . . . We find the Apostles endowed with greater power than John [the Baptist]: their office was more under the spirit and power of Elijah than Elias."[3]

Thus, the name "Elias" in the New Testament may refer to someone who has the calling of a forerunner, preparer, or restorer; to the actual Old Testament person named Elias; or to Elijah. The Joseph Smith Translation clarifies that, of the fifteen references to Elias in the New Testament, four of them—namely Matthew 11:13–14; 17:10–13; Mark 9:11–13; and John 1:19–28—are referring to persons with the calling of Elias. These references are all to preparers or restorers and not to the person Elijah himself. John the Baptist is specifically designated as an Elias in all four scriptures.

Several other New Testament references to Elias definitely refer to Elijah. Consider, for instance, the reference by James to Elias's prayer for rain (see James 5:17), and by Paul to the Lord's answer to the prophet Elias that there were yet seven thousand in Israel who had not yet bowed the knee to Baal (see Romans 11:2–4). Jesus' own comments regarding Elias and the widow of Sarepta—Zarephath in the Old Testament—also refer to Elijah (see Luke 4:24–26). Several other references to Elias hint at the widespread public anticipation of Elijah's return. Herod Antipus—the slayer of John the Baptist—was curious as to the identity of Jesus because it was rumored by some "that Elias had appeared" (Luke 9:8). Similarly, when the Lord met with his disciples near Caesarea Philippi, he asked them, "Whom say the people that I am?" (Luke 9:18.) They responded that, among several possibilities, many thought him to be Elias, a probable reference to Elijah (see Luke 9:19; Matthew 16:14). This occasion elicited Peter's famous testimony: "Thou art the Christ, the Son of the living God" (Matthew 16:16).

Another important reference to Elijah occurred while Jesus hung on the cross and cried, "Eli, Eli, lama sabacthani?" (Matthew 27:46.) Several bystanders believed that he called for Elias. Jewish traditions recorded later in the Talmud indicate a strong belief that Elijah makes frequent appearances to assist the helpless. Those traditions probably already existed in the Lord's day, explaining why some at the cross said, "Let us see whether Elias will come to save him." (See Matthew 27:47–49.)

That leaves only two more New Testament instances of the use of the name Elias. The first is in Luke 1:17, where the angel Gabriel appeared to the priest Zacharias to tell him he would soon have a son named John who would be later designated "the Baptist." Gabriel said, "And he shall go before him in the spirit and power of Elias, to turn the hearts of the fathers to the children, and the disobedient to the wisdom of the just; to make ready a people prepared for the Lord." Here the mention of the spirit and power of Elias could refer either to Elias or to Elijah. The words "to turn the hearts of the fathers to the children" sound specifically like a quotation of Malachi's phrase about Elijah. The entire angelic prophecy can be read to refer to that which Elijah was foreordained to accomplish in the last days in preparing a people for the Lord's second coming. A footnote to the verse in the Latter-day Saint Edition of the King James Bible even indicates that Elias "is the Greek form of the Hebrew name, Elijah." Joseph Smith, however, indicated that John the Baptist's mission fit more under the spirit and power of Elias than Elijah, thereby agreeing with the four Joseph Smith Translation changes in the Gospels mentioned above.[4]

The verse in Luke might possibly indicate that John was destined to fulfill a dual role under the power of both Elias and Elijah, or that his mission would be a type of the mission to be performed by Elijah in the last days. However, there seems to be no other indication in our literature that John's calling was of a nature other than that of an Elias. Doctrine and Covenants 27:7 clarifies the issue, specifically stating that Zacharias was promised "that he should have a son, and his name should be John, and he should be filled with the spirit of Elias." Since the Lord referred to Elijah by name two verses later in the same revelation, clearly distinguishing between the two names, it seems apparent that the word Elias in Luke 1:17 should be grouped with those New Testament verses that we read as "Elias" as opposed to "Elijah." The only other references made to Elias in the Gospels are those that pertain to the events on the Mount of Transfiguration.

Chapter Fifteen

ELIJAH AND THE MOUNT OF TRANSFIGURATION

NOWHERE IN THE SCHOLARLY BIBLICAL literature concerning Elijah is there a greater lack of understanding than in those commentaries regarding his role in the New Testament. The regular academic world cannot accurately assess those references because it fails to grasp two significant concepts: (1) the existence of a person named Elias, and the role of his spirit as differentiated from that of Elijah (as discussed in chapter 14), and (2) the meaning of "the keys of the kingdom" (Matthew 16:19) and their relationship to Elijah's appearance on the Mount of Transfiguration.

Matthew 17:1–4; Mark 9:2–5; and Luke 9:28–33 contain the three accounts of the events on the Mount of Transfiguration, which events took place about a week after Peter's declaration at Caesarea Philippi that Jesus was the Christ (see Matthew 16: 13–20). Luke mentions that Jesus took the three Apostles Peter, James, and John "up into a mountain to pray" (Luke 9:28). Matthew observes that it was a "high mountain apart" (Matthew 17:1). From these descriptions, the two most likely candidates for the specific mountain where this event occurred are Mount Tabor, situated in the midst of the Jezreel valley, and Mount Hermon, located just north of the ancient city of Caesarea Philippi. While

95

each site has its adherents and its detractors, neither the exact placement of the mount nor all the details of what transpired there are significant for our discussion here. Our concern centers solely upon the coming of Elijah on that occasion.

Latter-day prophets have uniformly declared that the "Elias" who visited the Mount of Transfiguration was actually Elijah. In Doctrine and Covenants 138, President Joseph F. Smith referred to seeing in vision "Elias, who was with Moses on the Mount of Transfiguration" (v. 45). Lest there be any misunderstanding as to which person was meant, he continued in the following verses by speaking of Malachi, who had testified of the coming of Elijah, and briefly discussing the meaning of Elijah's coming (see vv. 46–48). It seems President Smith used the name Elias instead of Elijah simply because the New Testament account of the Transfiguration rendered it thus.

Why did Elijah come on that remarkable occasion? With only the brief New Testament accounts to rely on, most readers surmise that Moses came representing the law and Elijah the prophets. Both came to honor Christ and to speak "of his decease which he should accomplish at Jerusalem" (Luke 9:31). Their coming would also have deeply impressed upon the Apostles the realization of Jesus' true identity. The knowledge that the ancients knew and worshiped the same Holy One that the Apostles followed probably proved to be as powerful a witness of Jesus' messianic role as anything they had previously experienced. The display of the Lord's glory, the reverent, worshipful attitudes of Moses and Elijah, and the voice of the Father from heaven all contributed to the same end. The Apostles thus received three witnesses to Christ's divine sonship. While all of this accurately explains some of the reason behind Elijah's appearance, we must turn to latter-day revelation to gain a more in-depth understanding.

About a week before the events at the Mount of Transfiguration, Jesus promised Peter, "And I will give unto thee the keys of the kingdom of heaven: and whatsoever thou shalt bind on earth shall be bound in heaven: and whatsoever thou shalt loose on earth shall be loosed in heaven" (Matthew 16:19). Here the word *keys* has a powerful meaning. In general, a person possessing keys has some type of authority. Even today many persons in positions of authority in the Near East carry large numbers of keys. Key rings are often worn on the outside of garments, hanging from a belt or sash around the body or on a chain around the neck, so that they may be visible to everyone. The person who carries such keys is recognized as one who has authority in society.

In Matthew 16:19, the Savior used the word *keys* in a symbolic way to indicate the holding of authority from God, similar to the way the word had been used previously by Isaiah (see Isaiah 22:22). As a person with a literal key can open or shut a door, so one with "keys" of authority in God's kingdom can symbolically open or shut the doors of heaven by exercising his authority to bind (or seal) or loose on earth and in heaven. The word *seal* also signifies the placing of a stamp of approval on something. Accordingly, Elder Joseph Fielding Smith wrote: "These keys of the binding, or sealing power, which were given to Peter, James, and John in their dispensation, are keys which make valid *all* the ordinances of the gospel. They pertain more especially to the work in the temples, both for the living and for the dead. They are the authorities which prepare men to enter the celestial kingdom and to be crowned as sons and heirs of God."[1] In essence, as Elder Boyd K. Packer expressed it, these "keys of priesthood authority represent the limits of the power extended from beyond the veil to mortal man to act in the name of God upon the earth."[2]

To further understand the nature of Elijah's mission on the Mount of Transfiguration, we need to move forward in time to the glorious manifestation received by Joseph Smith and Oliver Cowdery in the Kirtland Temple on April 3, 1836. First, the Lord himself appeared to accept the temple, which had been dedicated the previous week. Then, in succession, Moses, Elias, and Elijah appeared to confer their keys upon Joseph and Oliver. Moses, known as the great lawgiver, had gathered the children of Israel when they were in bondage in Egypt; led them to Sinai, where the Lord established his covenant with them; and called them to be "a kingdom of priests, and an holy nation" (Exodus 19:6). Having been translated like Elijah,[3] he returned to earth at Kirtland to bestow on Joseph and Oliver the keys of the gathering of Israel, giving them authority to gather scattered Israel in the latter days (see D&C 110:11). Elias then restored "the dispensation of the gospel of Abraham" (D&C 110:12). Following those visitations, Elijah appeared and bestowed "the keys of this dispensation" (D&C 110:16). These keys that Elijah brought, those of the sacred sealing power, enable their bearer to seal on earth and in heaven and to loose on earth and in heaven, and are equated with the keys of the kingdom of God on earth. To summarize, these keys held by Elijah are, to use Elder Packer's words, "the consummate authority on this earth for man to act in the name of God."[4]

With this background, it seems clear that Moses and Elijah, the ancient guardians of their respective keys, would have bestowed the same keys on Peter, James, and John on the Mount of Transfiguration. After the Lord's resurrection, these three Apostles presided over the Church. Consequently, they needed the keys held by Moses in order to gather the Lord's people to the sacred covenant in their day, and those of Elijah to render all gospel covenants and ordinances binding throughout both mortal life and eternity. Joseph Smith stated that whenever the Lord has given the priesthood to men in any dispensation, "this power [the sealing power] has always been given" (D&C 128:9). The Lord had promised the Apostles this sealing power just a week before. They received it from Elijah on the Mount of Transfiguration.

It becomes apparent that Elijah had been translated to accomplish this express mission. He needed a physical body with tangible hands in order to lay his hands on the heads of Peter, James, and John. The same reasoning also explains Moses' translation and return. Neither could have then appeared as a resurrected being, for the first resurrection had not yet begun. We can only wonder whether the man Elias was not also there, and perhaps others.

But why did the ancient prophets come when the Lord Jesus could have bestowed the keys himself? After all, they were bestowing *his* priesthood and the keys of *his* power. Note that the same circumstances prevailed at Kirtland in 1836. On both occasions, the Lord was present but allowed the ancient prophets to bestow the keys. From this we see that the Lord's kingdom is one of order. He had ordained those prophets to hold those specific keys and honored them in having them bestow those keys in both instances. Even though the authority they held originally came from him, he allowed them to fulfill their stewardship by assigning them to pass their authority on to others. This presents a significant lesson we need to understand. The Lord allocates to his chosen messengers, be they angelic or mortal, the duties of administering his kingdom and lets them carry out their divine mandate. He works by delegation.

Similar examples are seen in the conversion of Paul and the life of Joseph Smith. Even though the Lord appeared to Paul on the road to Damascus, he sent Paul to Ananias for baptism rather than doing it himself. The Lord likewise appeared to Joseph Smith in person, but Joseph's subsequent training, his receipt of ordinances, and, ultimately, his receipt of priesthood keys came from the ancient prophets who had been given such responsibilities. Joseph learned much about the linking of dispensations from those experiences. He also learned that those who have already passed through this stage of existence continue to be involved and interested in the affairs of this earth.

Since Elijah was the prophet to whom the Lord delegated the authority to bestow the sealing power on the heads of subsequent generations, he was present at the Mount of Transfiguration. His bestowal of keys on Peter, James, and John validated all ordinances and covenants performed under their hands, thus ushering in the fulness of the holy priesthood in the meridian of time.

Chapter Sixteen

THE PROMISE OF ELIJAH'S RETURN RENEWED

WITHIN A FEW SHORT MONTHS FOLLOWING the events on the Mount of Transfiguration, that Personage whom Elijah served and honored, namely the Lord Jesus Christ, entered a garden named Gethsemane and underwent the suffering that wrought the infinite and eternal Atonement. At Christmas, we sing a carol that says, "The hopes and fears of all the years are met in thee tonight."[1] While these words fit the events of Jesus' birth in Bethlehem, they seem even more appropriate in referring to the drama that unfolded in Gethsemane. That sacred night and the subsequent Crucifixion must surely have been the focus of attention for all of God's creations.

Jesus' final words from the cross triumphantly signaled, "Father, it is finished, thy will is done" (JST, Matthew 27:54). At the same moment that Jerusalem, the holy city, experienced darkness and earthquake and the rending of the sacred veil of its temple, the spirit of the Holy One, whose lifeless form hung on the cross, pierced another veil, separating this mortal sphere from the spirit world. There the spirits of righteous men and women of ages past anxiously awaited the arrival of their Lord and Master.

As President Joseph F. Smith pondered over the Apostle Peter's words regarding Christ's visit to the spirit world, he received a glorious vision of that unique event, as recorded in Doctrine and Covenants 138. President Smith saw that "there were gathered together in one place an innumerable company of the spirits of the just, who had been faithful in the testimony of Jesus while they lived in mortality" (v. 12). When he came among them, Jesus "preached to them the everlasting gospel, the doctrine of the resurrection and the redemption of mankind from the fall, and from individual sins on conditions of repentance" (v. 19). As he had called and sent forth messengers of these glad tidings on the earth, he also gathered the righteous in the spirit world and "organized his forces and appointed messengers, clothed with power and authority, and commissioned them to go forth and carry the light of the gospel to them that were in darkness, even to all the spirits of men; and thus was the gospel preached to the dead. . . . These were taught faith in God, repentance from sin, vicarious baptism for the remission of sins, the gift of the Holy Ghost by the laying on of hands." (Vv. 30, 33.)

Amid the vast throng, President Smith saw Adam and Eve, the parents of all mankind, and many of their noble and faithful posterity. President Smith specifically mentioned others whom he saw:

> Elias, who was with Moses on the Mount of Transfiguration;
>
> And Malachi, the prophet who testified of the coming of Elijah—of whom also Moroni spake to the Prophet Joseph Smith, declaring that he should come before the ushering in of the great and dreadful day of the Lord—were also there.
>
> The Prophet Elijah was to plant in the hearts of the children the promises made to their fathers,
>
> Foreshadowing the great work to be done in the temples of the Lord in the dispensation of the fulness of times, for the redemption of the dead, and the sealing of the children to their parents, lest the whole earth be smitten with a curse and utterly wasted at his coming. (Vv. 45–48.)

It is interesting to note that both Elijah and Moses (see v. 41), who had met with the Lord a few months earlier on the Mount of Transfiguration, now mingled with the spirits in paradise. Apparently they had the ability in their translated state to interact with those in the spirit world, anticipating the appearance of the Savior and the time of resurrection.

As earthly time is measured, the Savior was only in the spirit world a short interval before reentering his physical tabernacle, which had lain inanimate in the tomb of Joseph of Arimathea. It was the morning of his resurrection, the perfecting of the Atonement. The promised Messiah had overcome both death and hell. As soon as Christ had "risen from the dead, and become the first-fruits of them that slept" (1 Corinthians 15:20), many of the Saints also arose (see Matthew 27:52). The first resurrection had thus begun. We might expect to find Elijah and others who had been previously translated among those risen Saints. Would they not have taken part in that first resurrection, their translated or terrestrial state being changed to a celestial one? The Doctrine and Covenants confirms this expectation, stating, "And from Moses to Elijah, and from Elijah to John, who were with Christ in his resurrection" (133:55). Hence Elijah, having completed both his Old Testament and New Testament assignments, rose in glory to await his future assignments, including his part in the opening stages of the last and greatest of all dispensations, the dispensation of the fulness of times.

Following the Resurrection, the Lord ministered among his Apostles and followers in Jerusalem and Galilee. He was seen of his disciples forty days, "speaking of the things pertaining to the kingdom of God" (Acts 1:3). Among his instructions to those to whom the keys of sealing had been given, the Lord surely would have discussed his visit to the spirit world, explaining how the door had been opened for the preaching of the gospel there and how the necessary ordinances of the gospel could now be performed vicariously for those who had already passed from this mortal sphere of existence. Those who held the keys to bind both on earth and in heaven needed to understand what was going on in both places. Peter's mention of Christ's visit to the spirit world (see 1 Peter 3:18–20; 4:6) and the obvious reference by Paul to baptisms for the dead being performed by the early Saints (see 1 Corinthians 15:29) both evidence that the Apostles understood these things.

Sometime after the Savior's resurrection, he also visited his followers in the western hemisphere. Centuries earlier, at the time of Jerusalem's destruction by the Babylonians, he led their forefathers from Jerusalem to the Americas. There they and their descendants established a great civilization, mighty in both righteousness and wickedness. Because of their wickedness many calamities fell upon them at the time of the Savior's crucifixion. Entire cities were destroyed. In the end, the Lord spared only the "more righteous" part of the people (3 Nephi 9:13). It was to this righteous remnant of the people known as the Nephites that the Lord made his wondrous appearance as recorded in 3 Nephi 11–28.

On the second day of his visit to this people, "after he had expounded all the scriptures unto them which they had received, he said unto them: Behold, other scriptures I would that ye should write, that ye have not" (3 Nephi 23:6). Included in those verses, the Savior gave them what we recognize as Malachi chapters 3 and 4. Because the ancestors of the Nephites had left Jerusalem almost two centuries before Malachi made his prophecies, the Nephites did not have a record of them. 3 Nephi 25:5–6 in the Book of Mormon reads the same as Malachi 4:5–6 in the King James Version of the Bible. After reciting these scriptures to the people, the Savior said, "These scriptures, which ye had not with you, the Father commanded that I should give unto you; for it was wisdom in him that they should be given unto future generations" (3 Nephi 26:2). He then explained all things to them "from the beginning until the time that he should come in his glory" (3 Nephi 26:3). It seems likely that, having just quoted these verses about Elijah's promised return, the Lord then explained something about Elijah's mission, what it meant and why it was necessary. Because that mission and the keys of the sealing power that form such an integral part of it pertain so much to the sacred work carried on in the holy temples of the Lord, it is not surprising that the text of 3 Nephi does not give us more detail about the Lord's explanations. They were probably things of such a sacred nature as to be learned by us only in the temple. The prophet-editor Mormon simply tells us that "there cannot be written in this book even a hundredth part of the things which Jesus did truly teach unto the people" (3 Nephi 26:6). Mormon also mentions that only the "lesser part of the things which [Jesus] taught the people" (v. 8) were written in order to test the faith of those of us who would receive this book in the latter days. Indeed, God expressly forbade Mormon to write more (see v. 11).

Since Mormon included so little of the Lord's sermons, it is significant that he recorded the entire text of Malachi chapters 3 and 4. The prophecies relative to the Lord's second coming that they contain must have been of special importance to him. Mormon probably would have known of Elijah's mortal ministry in ancient Israel because of the records contained on the plates of brass. The Savior likely explained to the Nephites more about that prophet's special ministry. Certainly the Lord instituted temple work for the living and the dead among the Nephites as he had done among his disciples in Jerusalem. We might even wonder if Elijah himself had at some time come to bestow keys upon the Nephites as he had upon the Apostles on the Mount of Transfiguration. All these things would have been known both by Mormon and by his son, Moroni. After the resurrected Lord's revelation of the plan of salvation—including the marvelous aspects of Elijah's mission—to his disciples in both hemispheres, the preaching of the glad tidings of gospel truth brought immense joy to numerous people. We suppose that the exercise of priesthood keys sealed the blessings of gospel ordinances upon many souls. With the passage of time, however, pride, iniquity, and false doctrine crept into the Church, eventually squeezing out truth and revelation. The dark night of the Apostasy settled over the entire world, awaiting the light of a new dawn.

Chapter Seventeen

THE DAWNING OF A
BRIGHTER DAY

The morning breaks, the shadows flee;
Lo, Zion's standard is unfurled!
The dawning of a brighter day
Majestic rises on the world.[1]

AFTER CENTURIES OF PREPARATION AND anticipation, the light of a brighter day dawned; the heavens opened to reveal their splendor early in the spring of 1820 in an obscure location in upstate New York. Centuries of darkness and ignorance were swept away by the brilliance of a visit from the realms of the eternities. In answer to the humble prayer of an earnest fourteen-year-old boy, Joseph Smith, God the Father and his Son, Jesus Christ, appeared in resplendent glory. The time had finally arrived for the "restitution of all things, which God hath spoken by the mouth of all his holy prophets since the world began" (Acts 3:21). Young Joseph Smith would be the Lord's instrument to bring about the prophesied restoration of all things.

Joseph wrote that following this miraculous visitation—the opening of a new dispensation of the gospel—he continued to pursue his "common vocations in life until the twenty-first of September, one thousand eight hundred and twenty-three" (Joseph Smith—History 1:27). The *Farmer's Almanac* printed in Ithaca, New York, for the year 1823 indicates that on that date the weather would have been warm and the moon full.[2] The 21st fell on Sunday—the Lord's day—during the time of the autumnal equinox, when the hours of daylight and darkness are roughly equal in duration. Concerning that day, Joseph recorded: "I betook myself to prayer and supplication to Almighty God for forgiveness of all my sins and follies, and also for a manifestation to me, that I might know of my state and standing before him; for I had full confidence in obtaining a divine manifestation, as I previously had one. While I was thus in the act of calling upon God, I discovered a light appearing in my room, which continued to increase until the room was lighter than at noonday, when immediately a personage appeared at my bedside, standing in the air, for his feet did not touch the floor." (Joseph Smith—History 1:29–30.)

Joseph's record continues with his description of the angelic being who stood before him, providing us the most detailed portrayal of a resurrected person other than the Lord to be found in our scriptures. Joseph then recounted, "He called me by name, and said unto me that he was a messenger sent from the presence of God to me, and that his name was Moroni; that God had a work for me to do" (Joseph Smith—History 1:33). The personage at Joseph's bedside was the resurrected Moroni, who possessed "the keys of the record of the stick of Ephraim" (D&C 27:5). Moroni told Joseph of a book written on gold plates and described to him where it could be found. Joseph's subsequent translation of these plates by the gift and power of God we now know as the Book of Mormon. Moroni next quoted several Old Testament prophecies. Joseph's account states:

> He first quoted part of the third chapter of Malachi; and he quoted also the fourth or last chapter of the same prophecy, though with a little variation from the way it reads in our Bibles. Instead of quoting the first verse as it reads in our books, he quoted it thus:
>
> For behold, the day cometh that shall burn as an oven, and all the proud, yea, and all that do wickedly shall burn as stubble; for

they that come shall burn them, saith the Lord of Hosts, that it shall leave them neither root nor branch.

And again, he quoted the fifth verse thus: Behold, I will reveal unto you the Priesthood, by the hand of Elijah the prophet, before the coming of the great and dreadful day of the Lord.

He also quoted the next verse differently: And he shall plant in the hearts of the children the promises made to the fathers, and the hearts of the children shall turn to their fathers. If it were not so, the whole earth would be utterly wasted at his coming. (Joseph Smith—History 1:36–39.)

Moroni recited various other verses of scripture to seventeen-year-old Joseph, but it is significant that he first quoted these verses of Malachi predicting the return of Elijah. Moroni returned twice more that night and again the next morning, each time quoting the very same verses in the same way. What a powerfully deep impression those verses about the return of Elijah must have made on young Joseph's mind! Yet it would be many years before he began to fully understand their message.

There is no need here to review Joseph's visits to Cumorah, his tutoring by the prophet Moroni, nor the translation of the plates and the publication of the Book of Mormon. Nor is there need to discuss the many other momentous events of Joseph's young life, including the miraculous visitations of other angelic ministers, Joseph's marriage to Emma Hale, the many moves and persecutions he endured. Those are all treated at length in other books and articles.[3]

The restoration of the priesthood does warrant mention because of the nature of Elijah's power and mission. Joseph Smith wrote that on the 15th of May, 1829, he and his scribe in translation, Oliver Cowdery, in the course of translating the Book of Mormon,

> went into the woods to pray and inquire of the Lord respecting baptism for the remission of sins, that we found mentioned in the translation of the plates. While we were thus employed, praying and calling upon the Lord, a messenger from heaven descended in a cloud of light, and having laid his hands upon us, he ordained us, saying:

Upon you my fellow servants, in the name of Messiah, I confer the Priesthood of Aaron, which holds the keys of the ministering of angels, and of the gospel of repentance, and of baptism by immersion for the remission of sins; and this shall never be taken again from the earth until the sons of Levi do offer again an offering unto the Lord in righteousness. (Joseph Smith—History 1:68–69.)

The messenger "said that his name was John, the same that is called John the Baptist in the New Testament, and that he acted under the direction of Peter, James and John, who held the keys of the Priesthood of Melchizedek, which Priesthood, he said, would in due time be conferred on us" (Joseph Smith—History 1:72). One result of the long era of apostasy was that no living mortal held authority to officiate in the ordinances of the priesthood. That situation necessitated John's visit. At his direction, Joseph and Oliver baptized and ordained each other. The power of the Aaronic Priesthood was again upon the earth. Sometime during the following month, Peter, James, and John also visited Joseph Smith just as John the Baptist predicted. Holding the keys of the Melchizedek Priesthood, the ancient presidency conferred the Melchizedek Priesthood upon Joseph and Oliver and ordained them Apostles. (See D&C 20:2–3; 27:12.)

With the power and authority of this higher priesthood, Joseph Smith possessed the ability to formally organize the Church of Christ. As directed by the Lord, that special event took place in Fayette, New York, on April 6, 1830. In the course of that organizational meeting, the Lord designated Joseph Smith as "a seer, a translator, a prophet, an apostle of Jesus Christ" (D&C 21:1). With the translation of the Book of Mormon, the restoration of the power of the Melchizedek Priesthood, and the organization of the Church accomplished, missionaries bearing the glad news of the Restoration sought to proclaim it near and far. Many people seeking to know the truth joined the fledgling body of Church members as the Holy Spirit inspired them to do so. Gradually, the Church's tiny congregation grew in numbers and strength. The message of the Restoration spread to ever-widening circles, and many were drawn to its light.

Doctrine and Covenants 29:7–8 contains the first reference to the responsibility of the Church to "gather" to a certain location: "And ye are called to bring to pass the gathering of mine elect; for mine elect hear my voice and harden not their hearts: wherefore the decree hath gone forth from the Father that they shall be gathered in unto one place upon the face of this land, to prepare their hearts and be prepared in all things against the day when tribulation and desolation are sent forth upon the wicked." That revelation was given in Fayette, New York, in September 1830. Just three months later, in December, the Lord commanded Joseph to "go to the Ohio" and that the Church "should assemble together at the Ohio" (D&C 37:1, 3), the first recorded location designated for gathering in this dispensation.

During this time, Joseph was busy receiving revelations, conducting conferences, sending forth missionaries, producing an inspired translation of the Bible, and avoiding persecution from his enemies. At a conference in Fayette in January 1831, the Lord explained the reason for going west to Ohio, stating that the wicked were plotting to destroy Joseph Smith and the Church (see D&C 38:11–13, 31–32). In this revelation the Lord indicated he would soon give his law to the Church. He fulfilled that promise in the revelation known as section 42, given February 9, 1831, in Ohio. In Fayette, the Lord also promised that, after going to the Ohio, the Saints would "be endowed with power from on high" (D&C 38:32). The Lord, therefore, desired his people to gather in Ohio so as to both protect them from persecution and grant them an "endowment," or gift, of power from on high.

The Church members began to gather in the area of Kirtland, Ohio. There the Lord revealed to the Prophet the "law of the Church," section 42, and revealed many other significant principles and doctrines. Indeed, the heavens were opened and Joseph received a veritable flood of revelations concerning both spiritual and temporal matters. In the relatively early stages of the gathering to Kirtland, the Lord also revealed that the ultimate place of gathering would be in Missouri (see D&C 57). Consequently, on the third of August, 1831, Joseph Smith and several of the brethren met at a spot a little west of the courthouse in Independence,

Jackson County, Missouri, and dedicated that site for the construction of the great temple of Zion to be built in the last days.[4] But even following the designation of that important place, the Lord chose to maintain Kirtland as a "stake" of Zion (D&C 82:14). The word *stake* comes from the writings of the prophet Isaiah, who pictorially described Zion as a tent held in place by numerous stakes (see Isaiah 54:2; 33:20).

The Lord's revelation regarding establishing a "school of the prophets" given in December 1842 foreshadowed the construction of the first temple of this dispensation in Kirtland, Ohio (see D&C 88). That school was to be a place of learning and revelation for those purified from the sins of the world. In June 1833, the Lord chastened the Saints for having not proceeded more expeditiously with building what he termed "mine house" (D&C 95:3). We can sense the importance of such an undertaking from his words: "Yea, verily I say unto you, I gave unto you a commandment that you should build a house, in the which house I design to endow those whom I have chosen with power from on high; for this is the promise of the Father unto you; therefore I command you to tarry, even as mine apostles at Jerusalem" (D&C 95:8–9). The Lord then revealed to Joseph the pattern of this first latter-day temple[5] (see D&C 95:13–17).

Actual construction of the temple began in June 1833—the very month that the Lord commanded it be erected. The cornerstones were laid July 23, 1833,[6] and construction continued throughout the next two and one-half years. The early Saints sacrificed much to complete the sacred edifice. As the building approached completion in early 1836, spiritual blessings and manifestations began to be poured out upon the Saints.

On Thursday, January 21, 1836, the First Presidency met with the patriarch Joseph Smith, Sr., in the temple attic, where they anointed and blessed one another. In the course of these blessings, the heavens opened and Joseph the Prophet "beheld the celestial kingdom of God, and the glory thereof." He viewed "the blazing throne of God, whereon was seated the Father and the Son." (D&C 137:1, 3.) Joseph saw Adam, Abraham, his own father and mother, and his deceased brother Alvin. Joseph stated that upon seeing his brother in the celestial kingdom, he "marveled" (v. 6), because Alvin, having died before the restoration of the gospel and the priesthood, had not been baptized. Joseph then recorded: "Thus came the voice of the Lord unto me, saying: All who have died without a knowledge of this gospel, who would have received it if they had been permitted to tarry, shall be heirs of the celestial kingdom of God; also all that shall die henceforth without a knowledge of it, who would have received it with all their hearts, shall be heirs of that kingdom" (D&C 137:7–8). The Prophet also learned "that all children who die before they arrive at the years of accountability are saved in the celestial kingdom of heaven" (D&C 137:10).

Note the significance of the Lord's revealing these important doctrines to Joseph in the context of his own family. Joseph saw his father and mother in the celestial kingdom, even though they were then still living; indeed Joseph's father was with him on the occasion of the vision! Rather than being taught the great doctrine regarding the redemption of the dead in some abstract way, Joseph saw his own deceased brother Alvin enjoying the blessings of celestial life. Joseph acknowledged the reality of what he had seen, although he probably failed to fully understand the method and power the Lord would employ to bring about those blessings. In other words, the full import of Elijah's mission had not yet been revealed to Joseph. He certainly remembered Moroni's words and knew that Elijah's mission had something to do with families, with turning the hearts of fathers to children and the hearts of children to fathers. But on that January 21, Joseph received the additional insight that all who would have fully accepted the gospel will receive celestial blessings. Perhaps the Lord's words about "children who die before they arrive at the years of accountability [being] saved in the celestial kingdom of heaven" (D&C 136:10) were even related to the Prophet's concern about the children born to him and Emma who had previously died. What better way to prepare the Prophet for Elijah's coming than by relating Elijah's mission to Joseph's own family?

The long-awaited day of dedication for the Kirtland Temple arrived on Sunday, March 27, 1836. The Saints gathered early in the morning and the dedicatory service began at 9:00 A.M. The crowd was so great that they held a second such meeting the following Thursday for those unable to gain entrance on Sunday morning. The service continued for several hours. Its high point was the prayer of dedication, which the Prophet received by revelation (see D&C 109). That prayer expressed thanksgiving for the Lord's blessings and then prayed that this temple, constructed by his people, would be acceptable to him. Following the prayer, the congregation sang "The Spirit of God," a hymn written by William W. Phelps specifically for the temple dedication, and partook of the sacrament. The service then concluded with the sacred Hosanna Shout. That evening a special meeting for priesthood holders also took place. The entire day was one of a pentecostal outpouring of the Spirit. The "sound of a rushing mighty wind" filled the temple. People prophesied, spoke in tongues, and saw angels.[7] At last, "a house of God" (D&C 88:119) had been constructed and dedicated according to the Lord's direction. This temple had been erected "that the Son of Man might have a place to manifest himself to his people" (D&C 109:5). The anticipated manifestations began when the Lord appeared just seven days later.

Chapter Eighteen

THE VISITATION OF ELIJAH AT KIRTLAND

SUNDAY, APRIL 3, 1836, REMAINS ONE of the most momentous days in the history of this earth. For the first time in many centuries, the Lord visited his temple, the temple that his people had prayerfully dedicated to him one week earlier. April 3 fell on both Easter Sunday, the day celebrating Christ's resurrection, and the weekend of Passover, when Jews worldwide celebrated the deliverance of their forefathers from bondage in Egypt.[1] Thanks to ancient traditions that linked Elijah's coming to the time of Passover, the scattered Jews had awaited the arrival of Elijah at that special season for several centuries. While their expectation as to the timing of his arrival proved to be accurate, he did not come to the homes of those observing Passover. Instead, he visited the house of God reared by the Latter-day Saints in Kirtland, Ohio.

After the Sunday afternoon service in the temple, Joseph Smith, accompanied by Oliver Cowdery, went behind the Melchizedek Priesthood pulpit on the west end of the building to pray. They lowered a veil or curtain to be afforded privacy. Following prayer, they experienced the remarkable visitations recorded in Doctrine and Covenants section 110. First, the Lord appeared before them in glory. He introduced himself, forgave their sins, and declared:

Let the hearts of your brethren rejoice, and let the hearts of all my people rejoice, who have, with their might, built this house to my name.

For behold, I have accepted this house, and my name shall be here; and I will manifest myself to my people in mercy in this house.

Yea, I will appear unto my servants, and speak unto them with mine own voice, if my people will keep my commandments, and do not pollute this holy house.

Yea the hearts of thousands and tens of thousands shall greatly rejoice in consequence of the blessings which shall be poured out, and the endowment with which my servants have been endowed in this house.

And the fame of this house shall spread to foreign lands; and this is the beginning of the blessing which shall be poured out upon the heads of my people. Even so. Amen. (D&C 110:6–10.)

After that vision closed, Moses, the ancient lawgiver, appeared in order to bestow the "keys of the gathering of Israel from the four parts of the earth, and the leading of the ten tribes from the land of the north" (v. 11). He was followed by a prophet named Elias, who "committed the dispensation of the gospel of Abraham, saying that in us and our seed all generations after us should be blessed" (v. 12). Last of all came Elijah, saying, "Behold, the time has fully come, which was spoken of by the mouth of Malachi—testifying that he [Elijah] should be sent, before the great and dreadful day of the Lord come—to turn the hearts of the fathers to the children, and the children to the fathers, lest the whole earth be smitten with a curse—therefore, the keys of this dispensation are committed into your hands; and by this ye may know that the great and dreadful day of the Lord is near, even at the doors" (vv. 14–16).

Thus, following the Lord's appearance, three of his special servants came, each bestowing a special blessing or endowment of power and authority. The Lord himself certainly could have granted these blessings, since he is the source of all goodness and power. But, as previously discussed, he delegates. Therefore, Moses came to bestow keys—those rights of presidency, of presiding authority—concerning the gathering of scattered Israel. Then, as Elder Joseph Fielding Smith wrote, "Elias came, after Moses had conferred his keys, and brought the gospel of the dispensation in which Abraham lived. Everything that pertains to that dispensation, the blessings that were conferred upon Abraham, the promises that were given to his posterity, all had to be restored, and Elias, who held the keys of that dispensation, came."[2] Last of all came Elijah in fulfillment of all the prophecies that foretold his coming before the great and dreadful day of the Lord. He did not institute something new in turning the hearts of the fathers and the children, but, as part of the restoration of all things, he merely restored something that had disappeared during the era of apostasy. Specifically, he came to restore God's children to their previously existing relationships with one another and with their Heavenly Father.

In accomplishing that mission, Elijah granted unto Joseph Smith "the keys of this dispensation" (D&C 110:16). Elder Joseph Fielding Smith wrote: "The Lord gave unto Elijah the keys of presidency in his time—the keys of the kingdom, the keys of the sealing power; and it is that sealing power which gave him the right and authority to officiate. And the Lord said unto him, 'That which you bind on earth shall be bound in heaven.' That is how great his power was, and in that day Elijah stood up and officiated for the people in the sealing power."[3] This helps explain why, as Elder Bruce R. McConkie stated, "for three thousand years, instead of speaking of him [Elijah] as *a* prophet, he has always been known as *the* prophet."[4] The Prophet Joseph Smith said: "Elijah was the last Prophet that held the keys of the Priesthood, and who will, before the last dispensation, restore the authority and deliver the keys of the Priesthood, in order that all the ordinances may be attended to in righteousness. It is true that the Savior had authority and power to bestow this blessing; but the sons of Levi were too prejudiced. 'And I will send Elijah the Prophet before the great and terrible day of the Lord.' etc., etc. Why send Elijah? Because he holds the keys of the authority to administer in all the ordinances of the Priesthood; and without the authority is given, the ordinances could not be administered in righteousness."[5]

Although Joseph said that "Elijah was the last Prophet that held the keys of the Priesthood," it appears that others after

Elijah's time also held some keys that validated the gospel ordinances effected during their administrations. Consider the prophets of ancient Israel who followed Elijah and those among the Nephites. Did they not need priesthood keys to properly fulfill their prophetic responsibilities? And what of the specific reference made in Helaman 10 about the bestowal of the sealing power upon Nephi, the son of Helaman? Perhaps Joseph meant that Elijah was the last to hold *all* the keys, or that he was the last prophet to hold the fulness of the keys of the priesthood over *all* the tribes of Israel before the Lord began to scatter them in the eighth century B.C. Or maybe Joseph meant that Elijah is the last prophet holding the keys of the priesthood who would come to restore them. Whatever the full meaning of Joseph's statement may be, Elijah clearly was the one chosen to restore those keys in this last dispensation, just as he had restored them to Peter, James, and John. The Prophet Joseph's statement further signifies that, without the authority possessed by Elijah, "the ordinances could not be administered in righteousness." This indicates that anyone who professes to administer saving ordinances without possessing the sealing power restored by Elijah does so in unrighteousness and renders the ordinances invalid.

A deeper consideration of Elijah's coming reveals another profound reason for his return. Just as Peter, James, John, and their nine companions were ordained as Apostles early in Jesus' ministry, long before the bestowal of keys to the three on the Mount of Transfiguration, Joseph was also ordained an Apostle long before Elijah's visit. In both cases, the bestowal of the keys to seal and bind on earth and in heaven seems to have been the final endowment of power to act in the Lord's behalf on earth given to the leaders of his church. It may be that part of Elijah's coming was, in the words of Malachi's prophecy as quoted by Moroni, to "reveal unto you the Priesthood" (Joseph Smith—History 1:38), or to reveal *how* the priesthood should be administered, to make known dimensions of its power and dominion beyond what had been previously comprehended. Also, if, as Elder Joseph Fielding Smith indicated, the sealing power bestowed by Elijah places the Lord's "stamp of approval upon every ordinance that is done in this

Church and more particularly those that are performed in the temples of the Lord,"6 that would indicate that ordinances performed by the Church before Elijah's visit awaited that stamp of approval. In confirmation of that, Elder Boyd K. Packer has stated: "Thirteen years after Moroni appeared, a temple had been built adequate for the purpose, and the Lord again appeared and Elijah came with Him and bestowed the keys of the sealing power. Thereafter ordinances were not tentative, but permanent. The sealing power was with us. No authorization transcends it in value. That power gives substance and eternal permanence to all ordinances performed with proper authority for both the living and the dead."7 The time of tentativeness was over; the time of permanence had arrived.

Similarly, the gathering of the Saints before Moses restored the keys pertaining to gathering had been fairly slow and comparatively small. Following his visitation, the Church sent missionaries to Great Britain and the great gathering began, first to Nauvoo and then to the valleys of the West. As to both the scope and speed of gathering and the validity of eternal ordinances, all that occurred prior to the bestowal of the respective keys in Kirtland seems to have been only preliminary. Remember that the Lord did not bestow the keys upon Peter, James, and John at the time of their original ordination. The ordinances they originally performed must have also waited for final approval or permanence until they received the sealing keys.

Some have wondered why Peter, James, and John did not bestow the keys of the sealing power on Joseph Smith in 1829. The ancient Apostles undoubtedly possessed those keys and had as much priesthood as Elijah. But it is one thing to have keys and quite another to be chosen to bestow them. The Lord gave the latter privilege to Elijah. The same holds true for Moses, as the Lord reserved the responsibility of restoring the keys of gathering specifically to him. Suffice it to say that in both dispensations the Lord commissioned Elijah to bring those consummate keys.

What else happened at Kirtland that day? Were other angels present? For that matter, had others also been present at the Mount of Transfiguration? Elder Joseph Fielding Smith indicated that he believed Peter, James, and John "received their endowments on the mount."[8] Did something similar occur to Joseph at Kirtland? Would one be given all the keys of the priesthood without being endowed? Our records indicate that up to that time only preliminary aspects of what we now know as the endowment had been administered. Was more then revealed to the Prophet?

As brief as Doctrine and Covenants section 110 is, it tells us all we need to know. And as for Elijah, his appearance and ministration fulfilled the prophecy recorded in all four of our standard works (see Malachi 4:5–6; 3 Nephi 25:5–6; D&C 2:1–3; Joseph Smith—History 1:38–39).

Over a year after these glorious events took place at Kirtland on that Easter Sunday, the Lord addressed the leaders of his Church: "For unto you, the Twelve, and those, the First Presidency, who are appointed with you to be your counselors and your leaders, is the power of this priesthood given, for the last days and for the last time, in the which is the dispensation of the fulness of times. Which power you hold, in connection with all those who have received a dispensation at any time from the beginning of the creation; for verily I say unto you, the keys of the dispensation, which ye have received, have come down from the fathers, and last of all, being sent down from heaven unto you." (D&C 112:30–32.) As we have seen, those holding keys truly *had* come: Moroni; John the Baptist; Peter, James, and John; Moses; Elias; and Elijah. But why did so many angelic ministers from so many past ages all converge at one time and place, and upon one person, the Prophet Joseph Smith? All their keys, powers, and glories flowed into this latter-day era and to its prophet to create the fulness needed in this dispensation to prepare the world for the Savior's second coming. As the Lord explained, "For therein are the keys of the holy priesthood ordained, that you may receive honor and glory" (D&C 124:34). The restoration of all things for the eventual honor and glory of the children of God was at last under way.

Chapter Nineteen

LINE
UPON LINE

THOUGH UNNOTICED BY THE WORLD, the coming of Elijah to Kirtland and his bestowal of the sealing keys of the priesthood were events that affect all who have lived or will yet live in this world. Yet, even after the bestowal and receipt of this power, it does not seem that Joseph Smith had a full realization of the significance of what had occurred. His visionary understanding of the breadth of this power, evidenced by his well-known sermon given in Nauvoo, Illinois, on March 10, 1844, did not materialize instantaneously. During the almost eight years between Elijah's appearance at Kirtland and the famous sermon, it appears Joseph's understanding of this sublime doctrine grew "here a little, and there a little" (Isaiah 28:10), in accordance with the Lord's promise, "For [I] will give unto the faithful line upon line, precept upon precept; and I will try you and prove you herewith" (D&C 98:12).

Up until the time of Elijah's arrival, the Church primarily had been developing organizationally, in quorums and congregations. Elijah's mission to "turn the heart of the fathers to the children, and the heart of the children to their fathers" (Malachi 4:6) dramatically altered the direction of the Church from that time forward by laying a doctrinal foundation that shifted the course of the Church toward the family. The sealing power turned the key to unlock the door to the exaltation of the family unit. The Church, thereafter, became a temple-building church in order to seal together families, not congregations. Perhaps Joseph Smith first glimpsed this new doctrinal direction when he received a vision of the celestial kingdom in the Kirtland Temple on January 21, 1836. There he saw *the* fathers, Adam and Abraham, and also his own father, mother, and brother. This vision of his family probably helped prepare him for Elijah's coming to turn the hearts of all families.

Joseph's initial understanding of the promise of Elijah's return may have caused the Prophet to think along the line of caring for our family members. Moroni added a new dimension to that understanding with an additional phrase, saying that Elijah would "plant in the hearts of the children the promises made to the fathers" (Joseph Smith—History 1:39) before the children's hearts would turn. This added statement indicates that the turning of hearts would have something to do with a newfound awareness of the covenants made with *the* fathers of old—the patriarchs—and of our relationship with them as well as with our more immediate fathers. While speaking in reference to the promise of Elijah's coming, Joseph said, "Now, the word *turn* here should be translated *bind*, or seal."[1] Both of these words denote permanent attachment. In this case, they signify being attached both to the covenants and to the people involved. As to the prophecy of Elijah's return, Joseph remarked, "In the end [the earth] shall be burned and few men left [see Isaiah 24:6]. But before that, God shall send unto them Elijah the prophet, and he shall reveal unto them the covenants of the fathers with relation to the children and the covenants of the children in relation to the fathers, that they may have the privilege of entering into the same, in order to effect their mutual salvation."[2]

Joseph's recorded discourses indicate that his understanding of the meaning of Elijah's mission apparently moved from "turning hearts" to "planting promises" to "binding or sealing." This progression seems symbolic of the order of the transmission of priesthood keys. Remember that Moses first restored the keys of gathering, symbolically turning us toward one another. Elias then brought all the promises and blessings incident to the Abrahamic covenant. Once the people were gathered, they could be taught and blessed, having the promises planted in their hearts. Elias's power was to draw us to the new and everlasting covenant of eternal marriage and to organize us in family units. However, his power and promises were conditional, as they needed the sealing power brought by Elijah to give formal approval to those marriages and those families, removing their conditional status and making them eternal. Hence, Joseph declared: "This power of Elijah is to that of Elias what in the architecture of the temple of God those who seal or cement the stone to their places are to those who cut or hew the stones, the one preparing the way for the other to accomplish the work. By this we are sealed with the Holy Spirit of Promise, i.e., Elijah."[3]

Returning to Church history, a review of events during the three years following the visitations at Kirtland in April 1836 reveals the hand of the adversary seeking to derail and destroy the Church. Imprisonments, mobbings, murders, financial distress, apostasy, and excommunications plagued the Church. Were not these persecutions an attempt by the adversary to stop the further understanding and implementation of all the keys and powers bestowed at Kirtland? But his plan failed. In the midst of those difficult days, the Lord inspired Joseph Smith to send the first missionaries to Great Britain. The keys brought by Moses were utilized in raising the gospel standard in that distant land and resulted in a flood of converts who accepted the message of the Restoration. Most of them descended from Ephraim, the son of Joseph who was sold into Egypt. Israel was being gathered in fulfillment of the ancient promises. In retrospect, we see that it was necessary to employ the keys of gathering first, before the keys of sealing could be fully exercised. As Joseph explained: "What was the object of gathering the Jews, or the people of God in any age of the world? . . . The main object was to build unto the Lord a house whereby He could reveal unto His people the ordinances of His house and the glories of His kingdom, and teach the people the way of salvation; for there are certain ordinances and principles that, when they are taught and practiced, must be done in a place or house built for that purpose."[4] The Saints were gathered so that they could build temples where their families could be sealed for eternity.

By May of 1839, Joseph was residing in Commerce, Illinois, which he later renamed Nauvoo. Both Saints who had been driven from Missouri and new converts flowed into the city. As time passed, the Lord gradually prepared them for the revelation of the full meaning of the keys Elijah had restored several years earlier. Then, on August 15, 1840, Joseph first preached the doctrine of baptism by proxy for one's dead ancestors who had not been privileged to receive the gospel during mortality. Joseph gave the discourse at the funeral of Seymour Brunson, a member of the Nauvoo high council. Simon Baker later recorded:

> I was present at a discourse that the prophet Joseph delivered on baptism for the dead 15 August 1840. He read the greater part of the 15th chapter of Corinthians and remarked that the Gospel of Jesus Christ brought glad tidings of great joy. . . . He also said the apostle [Paul] was talking to a people who understood baptism for the dead, for it was practiced among them. He went on to say that people could now act for their friends who had departed this life, and that the plan of salvation was calculated to save all who were willing to obey the requirements of the law of God. He went on and made a very beautiful discourse.[5]

The newly revealed doctrine was thrilling news to those who were spiritually receptive. For example, about a month following this sermon, Joseph Smith, Sr., passed away. Just before his death, he asked that someone be baptized for his deceased son Alvin. Hyrum fulfilled his father's request and was baptized by proxy in behalf of Alvin.[6]

Joseph continued teaching the doctrine of baptism for the dead that fall in the Church's general conference and also referred to it in a letter to the Twelve dated December 15, 1840. In that letter, he said, "The Saints have the privilege of being baptized for those of their relatives who are dead, whom they believe would have embraced the Gospel, if they had been privileged with hearing it, and who have received the Gospel in the spirit, through the instrumentality of those who have been commissioned to preach to them while in prison."[7] The Saints were thrilled with this new doctrinal understanding and began performing baptisms.[8]

It is not surprising that the very same month the doctrine of baptism for the dead was first preached publicly the First Presidency indicated the time had come to build another temple to the Lord.[9] The Saints were then struggling to establish themselves after their losses in Missouri. Knowing their circumstances, the Lord stated in a January 1841 revelation that the ordinance of baptism for the dead was to be performed in a holy house erected for him and that "only in the days of your poverty" (D&C 124:30) would he allow the ordinance to be performed elsewhere. In the same revelation, he declared: "Build a house to my name, for the Most High to dwell therein. For there is not a place found on earth that he may come to and restore again that which was lost unto you, or which he hath taken away, even the fulness of the priesthood." (D&C 124:27–28.)

This word *fulness* has great meaning. We refer to the era in which we live as the "dispensation of the fulness of times" (D&C 124:41), an era when the knowledge and powers of all past ages come together into a fulness or completeness. The word also refers to the blessings of the priesthood being made available to a fulness of people, meaning everyone who has ever lived. In its ultimate sense, *fulness* denotes the receipt of "all that [the] Father hath" (D&C 84:38), or exaltation and glory, "which glory shall be a fulness and a continuation of the seeds forever and ever" (D&C 132:19).

During the construction of the temple in Nauvoo, the Lord continued to instruct Joseph, line upon line, precept upon precept, until the fulness of priesthood blessings, covenants, and ordinances had been revealed so that exaltation might be made available to all of the Father's children. Elijah had restored all the power needed to complete Joseph's mission, but it took time and revelation for Joseph to fully understand how to use that power. Near the close of Joseph's mortal ministry, in his sermon at the partially completed temple, he insightfully observed, "Now for Elijah. The spirit, power, and calling of Elijah is, that ye have

power to hold the key of the revelations, ordinances, oracles, powers and endowments of the fulness of the Melchizedek Priesthood
and of the kingdom of God on the earth; and to receive, obtain,
and perform all the ordinances belonging to the kingdom of
God."[10] He further declared that "this is the difference between
the spirit and power of Elias and Elijah; for while the spirit of Elias
is a forerunner, the power of Elijah is sufficient to make our calling
and election sure."[11] Referring to the sealing of those on earth to
those beyond the veil, he concluded, "This is the power of Elijah
and the keys of the kingdom of Jehovah."[12] With this power now
fully understood and in use, the Lord had made all the covenants
and ordinances necessary for salvation and exaltation available to
his people.

Today, the sealing power and the ordinances flowing therefrom
remain in full force and effect in The Church of Jesus Christ of
Latter-day Saints. They continue to be available and administered
in holiness in the sacred houses of the Lord dedicated in many
lands. Those holy temples play a central role in Latter-day Saint
life. We go to them to receive sealing blessings for both the living
and the dead, and look to them to receive the fulness of God's
blessings made available by Elijah's return. In President Joseph
Fielding Smith's first address to the priesthood as President of the
Church on April 4, 1970, he affirmed:

> I do not care what office you hold in the Church—you may be an
> apostle, you may be a patriarch, a high priest, or anything else—but
> you cannot receive the fullness of the priesthood and the fullness of
> eternal reward unless you receive the ordinances of the house of the
> Lord; and when you receive these ordinances, the door is then open
> so you can obtain all the blessings which any man can gain.
>
>   . . . You can have [the fullness of the Lord's blessings] sealed
> upon you as an elder, if you are faithful; and when you receive them,
> and live faithfully and keep these covenants, you then have all that
> any man can get.
>
>   There is no exaltation in the kingdom of God without the full-
> ness of the priesthood.[13]

As noted by President Smith, the fulness of the priesthood comes only in the temple. Exaltation cannot exist without it. That is why temples stand at the center of the spiritual strength of both the Church and Latter-day Saint families. For that reason, President Howard W. Hunter requested that we make the temple "the great symbol of [our] membership."[14] That is why, as he said, we must point ourselves "toward [the Lord's] example and toward His temples."[15] And that is why each of us should seek to be enlivened by the "spirit of Elijah," so that in due course we may be able to receive that fulness.

Chapter Twenty

THE SPIRIT OF ELIJAH

THE PHRASE "SPIRIT OF ELIJAH" OCCURS only once in scripture, when the ancient prophet Elisha returned toward Jericho after having witnessed the translation of his predecessor, Elijah. The "sons of the prophets" said, "The spirit of Elijah doth rest on Elisha" (2 Kings 2:15). In the context of the discussion presented in the last two chapters, the word *spirit* used in this verse seems to be synonymous with *power*. As commonly used today, the phrase "power of Elijah" refers to the sealing power currently held by the First Presidency and the Quorum of the Twelve Apostles of The Church of Jesus Christ of Latter-day Saints, which gives eternal validity to all ordinances performed in the Church. It particularly refers to the ordinances performed in the holy temples.

The phrase "spirit of Elijah," however, enjoys a broader meaning that denotes the turning of the hearts of all people to their familial ties. In this context, the word *heart* refers to our innermost self and our deepest affections. Therefore, when our innermost thoughts and desires turn toward our family members, living or dead, we are said to feel the "spirit of Elijah." In the Church, we use the word *dead* only to signify those who have passed on from this mortal sphere to the spirit world. Elder Joseph Fielding Smith wrote: "I think sometimes we look at this work for the salvation of the dead rather narrowly. It is a wrong conception to think of the people for whom we are doing work in the temple of the Lord as being dead. We should think of them as *living*; and the living proxy but represents them in receiving the blessings which they should have received, and would have received *in this life*, had they been living in a gospel dispensation."[1]

In a vision of Brigham Young's in which he saw Joseph Smith nearly three years following Joseph's martyrdom, Joseph instructed: "Be sure to tell the people to keep the Spirit of the Lord; and if they will, they will find themselves just as they were organized by our Father in Heaven before they came into the world. Our Father in Heaven organized the human family, but they are all disorganized and in great confusion." Brigham Young continued: "Joseph then showed me the pattern, how they were in the beginning. This I cannot describe, but I saw it, and saw where the Priesthood had been taken from the earth and how it must be joined together, so that there would be a perfect chain from Father Adam to his latest posterity."[2] Only through Elijah's mission can such organization be established out of the confusion seen by President Young. For this reason, the "message of Elijah," or "temple work," has been called "the keystone of the Gospel Arch."[3]

Without the spirit and power brought by Elijah, the calamitous confusion of peoples so prevalent throughout history would continue, and "the whole earth would be utterly wasted at [the Lord's] coming" (D&C 2:3). The first verse of the fourth chapter of Malachi says, "For, behold, the day cometh, that shall burn as an oven; and all the proud, yea, and all that do wickedly, shall be stubble: and the day that cometh shall burn them up, saith the Lord of hosts, that it shall leave them neither root nor branch." Malachi foresaw that those who willfully reject Christ and the eternal life that he alone can offer will be left without either root or branch, which here symbolically represent ancestry and posterity. Elijah's mission thus pertains to roots and branches, or fathers and children. Who are the fathers? Abraham, Isaac, and Jacob and their families certainly fit, but so do all those who have gone before us, both those here and those in the spirit world. Who are the children? Both those of our posterity now living on the earth and those yet to be born. To be left without roots and branches signifies having all family ties severed and being left alone.

To follow Malachi's symbolism a little further, Christ indicated that he is the true vine (see John 15:1–5). The keys of gathering allow people, or branches, to be gathered to the vine. Similarly, the keys restored by Elias bring those gathered people to the covenants and ordinances of the gospel, thereby symbolically grafting them to the vine. As the vine, Christ binds all together and gives life to all who are attached to him, including both roots and branches. The sap of the vine might represent Christ's sacrificial blood, flowing through all and giving life through gospel covenants and ordinances. If the graft does not succeed or the branch brings forth evil fruit, the branch dies, is cut off, and is cast out. If, however, the grafted branches receive nourishment from the life-giving sap and grow and bear good fruit, the power of Elijah binds or seals them permanently to the vine. If individuals, families, or whole societies reject Christ, it remains impossible to form that binding link. The proud souls who do not wish to bow to his will and refuse to be a branch attached to him, desiring instead to go their own way, eventually become lost, for that which "seeketh to become a law unto itself . . . cannot be sanctified" (D&C 88:35). They can never bear good fruit, nor will life be found in them. Were it not for the restoration of the spirit and power of Elijah, none of the branches could be permanently bound to the vine and the whole world would suffer utter destruction. However, the earth will not be utterly wasted precisely because the Lord's people are readying themselves to meet him at his second coming by receiving the sealing ordinances in his holy temples.

Elijah's mission encompassed not only the bestowal of formal priesthood keys upon the Lord's prophets but also the pouring out upon the world of a spirit that would assemble and prepare a people for the Messiah by causing their hearts to turn lovingly to their families. The very presence of the keys Elijah brought emanates that spirit of love and kinship, and has the ability to draw out our hearts towards our loved ones. Responding to a question regarding the object of Elijah's mission, the Prophet Joseph Smith stated,

"The keys are to be delivered, the spirit of Elijah is to come, the Gospel to be established, the Saints of God gathered, Zion built up, and the Saints to come up as saviors on Mount Zion."[4] In this statement, he juxtaposed the priesthood keys and the spirit of Elijah. The latter flows naturally from the former. Similarly, he said, "The spirit of Elias is first, Elijah second, and Messiah last. Elias is a forerunner to prepare the way, and the spirit and power of Elijah is to come after, holding the keys of power, building the Temple to the capstone, placing the seals of the Melchisedec Priesthood upon the house of Israel, and making all things ready; then Messiah comes to His Temple, which is last of all."[5] Thus, Elijah's arrival marks the final preparations of the Lord's people in readiness for his glorious return.

This spirit of Elijah has touched people throughout the world. Elder Joseph Fielding Smith wrote: "*Before* the year 1836 there was very little, if any, research being made anywhere in this world in behalf of the dead. It is true that here and there some man may have been searching out a genealogical record, but what was his object? To prove title to some estate. There were no genealogical societies; there were no genealogical organizations."[6] What a change has occurred in the world since Elijah's return in 1836! Today genealogy is one of the most actively pursued hobbies worldwide, and genealogical societies flourish. The spirit of Elijah has truly turned people's hearts without regard to their nationality, race, or religion.

The presence of this spirit among the Latter-day Saints causes them to gather so that temples may be built. It then prompts them to attend the temples regularly to both worship God and perform saving ordinances for themselves and in behalf of their deceased loved ones. It also inspires them to search out and verify the records of their ancestors. Elder Joseph Fielding Smith noted:

The fathers are our dead ancestors who died without the privilege of receiving the gospel, but who received the promise that the time would come when that privilege would be granted them. *The children* are those now living who are preparing genealogical data and who are performing the vicarious ordinances in the temples.

The turning of the hearts of the children to the fathers is placing or planting in the hearts of the children that feeling and desire
which will inspire them to search out the records of the dead.
Moreover the planting of the desire and inspiration in their hearts is
necessary. This they must have in order that they might go into the
house of the Lord and perform the necessary labor for their fathers,
who died without a knowledge of the gospel, or without the privilege
of receiving the fulness of the gospel.[7]

The bestowal of Elijah's keys and the spirit emanating therefrom have thus not only unlocked the doors to exaltation in the
celestial kingdom but also unlocked our own hearts. Instead of desiring to enter that kingdom alone, the spirit of Elijah prompts us
to want to go there together with those we love most and teaches
us how that can be done. The keys he brought transform the *possibility* of an eternal family unit into a *reality*. Elder Joseph Fielding
Smith observed: "If you want salvation in the fullest, that is exaltation in the kingdom of God, so that you may become his sons
and his daughters, you have got to go into the temple of the Lord
and receive these holy ordinances which belong to that house,
which cannot be had elsewhere. No man shall receive the fulness
of eternity, of exaltation, alone; no woman shall receive that blessing alone; but man and wife, when they receive the sealing power
in the temple of the Lord, if they thereafter keep all the commandments, shall pass on to exaltation, and shall continue and become
like the Lord. And that is the destiny of men; that is what the
Lord desires for his children."[8] Speaking of the sacred sealing of a
man and a woman in eternal marriage, Elder Boyd K. Packer said,
"And the highest ordinances in the House of the Lord they receive together and equally or not at all!"[9] The keys of Elijah make
that supernal sealing possible; the spirit of Elijah motivates us to
seek it with all our hearts.

In summary, the spirit of Elijah is that still small voice that
whispers deep inside us the word *family*. It beckons to all of us,
"Come home." Come home from extraneous temporal concerns,
come home from worldly preoccupations, break off the consuming
material chains with which you are bound. Leave sin and error be-

hind and come home. Please, come home! That quiet yet powerful voice is both a call to be united forever with our earthly families and an invitation to attend a reunion with the family of God, our Eternal Father, and form part of his divine, eternal family. If your thoughts turn backward to the lives and deeds of parents, grand-parents, and unknown ancestors with feelings of warmth, grati-tude, and a desire to know them better and be bound to them by sacred covenants through eternal power, you are awakening to the spirit of Elijah. If your thoughts turn forward with love to siblings, children, grandchildren, and posterity, and to the covenants and promises which can bind you eternally to them, you are feeling the spirit of Elijah. If love and gratitude for the one with whom you have knelt at a sacred altar in a holy temple and with whom you have made solemn and eternal covenants overwhelm you, you are experiencing the spirit of Elijah. And if you do not currently enjoy any such feelings, you need to get on your knees and prayerfully plead for them until they come!

Chapter Twenty-One

WHITHER GOEST THOU, ELIJAH?

THE MISSION OF THE CHURCH OF JESUS Christ of Latter-day Saints is to bring all men and women to Christ. That mission revolves around three significant principles: (1) the gathering of the Saints, (2) the perfecting of the Saints, and (3) the redemption of the dead. The gathering is that part of the mission involved with the preaching of the gospel of Christ worldwide. The greatest part of this work of gathering, conducted under the keys Moses restored to Joseph Smith in the Kirtland Temple in 1836, will yet occur in the future. Similarly, the perfecting of the Saints, while currently under way, will largely see its fruition in the future as ever larger numbers gather, receive covenants and ordinances, and learn to "live by every word that proceedeth forth from the mouth of God" (D&C 84:44). The keys restored by Elias encourage all to come to the new and everlasting covenant and be perfected. The sealing keys brought by Elijah, giving permanence to all gospel ordinances and covenants, operate today under the direction of the President of the Church. Their use shall continue and expand as Church membership grows and as temple construction and utilization accelerate.

It is humbling to contemplate how the fulness of priesthood blessings will be made available to men and women of all nations, kindreds, tongues, and peoples because the Lord sent a simple, faithful messenger from ancient Israel and clothed him with great power. As Elijah dwelt in a cave on Mount Horeb over 2,800 years ago, the voice of the Lord asked him, "What doest thou here, Elijah?" (1 Kings 19:9.) So might we ask of him, "Whither goest thou, Elijah?" Having learned about his mortal mission and his post-mortal ministry in dispensations following his own, and having a glimmer of the meaning of the spirit of Elijah, we might query, "Where now, what next, thou prophet of the covenant? What does the future hold?"

As we reflect on Elijah's life and mission, we must also wonder where the spirit and power he bestowed is now leading us. We have some idea of the efforts being exerted on this side of the veil by those who have been touched by the spirit of Elijah. Our hearts are being turned ever more completely to our families. We yearn to be with them, to bless them, and to love them. The more we feel of that spirit, the closer we draw to our immediate family members and the more anxious we become to find the distant ones and help them. In the recent past, President Spencer W. Kimball initiated a period of accelerated temple construction and genealogical activity. He was followed by President Ezra Taft Benson, who set an example for us by attending the temple weekly and who instructed us in its meaning in his great discourse, "What I Hope You Will Teach Your Children About the Temple."[1] President Howard W. Hunter then asked that we make the temple the symbol of our membership. President Gordon B. Hinckley has already dedicated more temples than any other man in this dispensation, or probably any preceding one. As the pace of temple service increases, it seems that all we have thus far seen constitutes only the beginning of the fulfillment of the work initiated by the restoration of keys by Elijah. The greatest era of temple building and redemptive work still lies ahead.

President Brigham Young prophesied:

> You will enter into the Temple of the Lord and begin to offer up ordinances before the Lord for your dead. . . . Before this work is finished, a great many of the Elders of Israel in Mount Zion will become

pillars in the Temple of God, to go no more out: they will eat and drink and sleep there; and they will often have occasion to say— "Somebody came into the Temple last night; we did not know who he was, but he was no doubt a brother, and told us a great many things we did not before understand. He gave us the names of a great many of our forefathers that are not on record, and he gave me my true lineage and the names of my forefathers for hundreds of years back. He said to me, You and I are connected in one family: there are the names of your ancestors; take them and write them down, and be baptised and confirmed, and save such and such ones, and receive of the blessings of the eternal Priesthood for such and such an individual, as you do for yourselves." This is what we are going to do for the inhabitants of the earth. When I look at it, I do not want to rest a great deal, but be industrious all the day long; for when we come to think upon it, we have no time to lose.[2]

More recently, President Spencer W. Kimball stated: "The day is coming, not too far ahead of us when all the temples on this earth will be going day and night. There will be shifts and people will be coming in the morning hours and in the night hours and in the day hours, and we may reach the time when we will have no (temple) vacations. . . . There will be a corps of workers night and day almost to exhaustion, because of the importance of the work and the great number of people who lie asleep in the eternity and who are craving and needing the blessings we can bring them."[3] With the sense of urgency inspired by such comments, we sometimes wonder where we should start. Elder Boyd K. Packer wrote:

> Sometimes this work may become a little discouraging. How can we seek out all of our progenitors—and all the others? One day while pondering prayerfully on this matter I came to the realization that there is something that any one of us can do for all who have died. I came to see that any one of us, by himself, can care about them, all of them, and love them. That came as a great inspiration, for then I knew there was a starting point.
>
> Whatever the number, we can love them and desire to redeem them. Any one of us has within him the power to expand his concern to include them all. If a billion more are added, we can *care* about them also. At least we can do that.

If the assignment seems impossible, we must move ahead. If the process is tedious, we must move ahead anyway. If the records have been lost, if the obstacles and opposition seem overwhelming, we will move ahead anyway. When we determine to do as the Lord commands, we move ahead.[4]

Such are the statements of those whose vision of this work has truly been magnified by the spirit of Elijah.

As we reflect on all that is happening here, we cannot help but wonder what activities are occurring on the other side of the veil. Are the hearts of those in the spirit world turned toward us in fulfillment of the prophecies about Elijah's mission? Have they too felt that spirit? Concerning them (and specifically past Church leaders and faithful Saints), President Joseph F. Smith said: "I believe they are as deeply interested in our welfare today, if not with greater capacity, with far more interest behind the veil, than they were in the flesh. . . . I claim that we live in their presence, they see us, they are solicitous for our welfare, they love us now more than ever."[5] In 1958, Elder Spencer W. Kimball said the following at a family reunion of the descendants of his grandfather President Heber C. Kimball:

> When I was asked to say a few words tonight I wondered what Grandfather would say if he were here, and I decided to let him say what I think he might:
>
> I AM YOUR GRANDFATHER, HEBER C. KIMBALL. I am a very busy man on the other side of the veil. You know this veil is a little like modern glass which admits vision from one side but is opaque on the other. I can see you but cannot be seen by you. I saw the family association leaders busy preparing for this reunion and thought I would drop in.
>
> I bring you greetings from your grandmothers, the loveliest women in any world.
>
> I have been present with you many times, but you did not know. When each of your grandmothers was buried I came for her, and as my own children began to leave mortality I was not so far away. I came to take them and to welcome them to the world of spirits. They are all on that side now and some of my grandchildren are arriving. I have looked in at the family reunions each year and noted

those of my children who were loyal to and proud of their ancestry and cousins. I was never called on to speak before.

My beloved, I can stay but these few minutes. But remember that I, too, was successful in business, and I held high office in politics. I helped in building many communities and an empire. I had houses and lands, and livestock, but I left them all on the earth. I knew, as I hope you will know and realize, that money cankers, livestock dies, houses deteriorate, stocks and bonds may come to naught. But the things which I did not leave on earth were the eternal verities: my spirit, my knowledge of the divinity of the work of the Lord for which we of that generation sacrificed so much.

I want you to know that I KNOW that God lives and that His Church is here and that to observe every directive of God is the most important thing for you. I plead with you to "SEEK YE FIRST THE KINGDOM OF GOD AND HIS RIGHTEOUSNESS" and all other things will follow.[6]

The impression given in these lines by Elder Kimball, and similar expressions given by many others, is that those on the other side not only are interested in us but have some influence upon us. Elder Melvin J. Ballard remarked:

I have said that when any man or woman goes into this work [the work for the dead] earnestly the Lord will provide ways and means for them to obtain the information they seek. Our understanding will be opened and sources of knowledge will be made manifest. Why? Because the dead know a great deal more than we do about existing records.

Why is it that sometimes only one of a city or household receives the Gospel? It was made known to me that it is because of the righteous dead who had received the Gospel in the spirit world exercising themselves, and in answer to their prayers elders of the Church were sent to the homes of their posterity that the Gospel might be taught to them and through their righteousness they might be privileged to have a descendant in the flesh do the work for their dead kindred. I want to say to you that it is with greater intensity that the hearts of the fathers and mothers in the spirit world are turned to their children than that our hearts are turned to them.[7]

Elder John A. Widtsoe made this additional reassuring statement: "I have the feeling . . . that those who give themselves with all their might and main to this work receive help from the other side, and not merely in gathering genealogies. Whoever seeks to help those on the other side receives help in return in all the affairs of life."[8]

These are marvelous insights about what the spirit of Elijah means on both sides of the veil and where it is leading us. But as wonderful as all this is, we must turn from the spirit of Elijah to again consider Elijah himself. Once again, we ask, "Whither goest thou, Elijah?" As others who have held special stewardships in ages past have exhibited continuing interest in events happening in our world, we may expect that he is both looking on and actively participating in the scenes preparatory to the glorious second coming of the Savior. If the Millennium is to be a time devoted to the accomplishment of a monumental amount of temple work continually overseen and directed by the keys of the priesthood that Elijah restored,[9] will the prophet's interest and involvement not continue until all that is needful has been accomplished and, in Joseph Smith's words, "the Great Jehovah shall say the work is done"?[10] Where is Elijah now? Is he among those commissioned to preach the gospel in the spirit world? Or is he involved in verifying and recording details about the ordinances made possible by his bestowal of keys in 1836? Is he overseeing the work currently being carried on in the temples of the Church? Is he helping those who are actively searching for records of their departed loved ones? Is he involved in strengthening individual families throughout the world, preparing some for the blessings of sealing and helping others maintain covenants already made? Or is he participating in all of the above, while fulfilling other assignments that we cannot even now imagine?

He will undoubtedly attend the great meeting to be held at Adam-ondi-Ahman, where, as Joseph Smith explained, Adam "will call his children together and hold a council with them to prepare them for the coming of the Son of Man. He (Adam) is the father of the human family, and presides over the spirits of all men, and all that have had the keys must stand before him in this grand council."[11] He shall also be present at that momentous gathering where, the Lord promised, "I will drink of the fruit of the vine with you on the earth . . . ; and also with . . . Elijah, unto whom I have committed the keys of the power of turning the hearts of the fathers to the children, and the hearts of the children to the fathers, that the whole earth may not be smitten with a curse" (D&C 27:5, 6, 9).

Truly, the crowning achievement of Elijah's lengthy ministry will have been to "turn the hearts" of so many both to each other and, through the everlasting covenant, to the Lord their God. Referring to the prophet Moroni's wording of the promise of Elijah's return, John A. Widtsoe wrote, "The beginning and the end of the Gospel is written, from one point of view, in Section 2 of the Book of Doctrine and Covenants."[12] That statement cannot help but elicit a smile, for the wonderful message of the restored gospel affirms that because Elijah came as prophesied in section 2, there will be no end to gospel nor life nor family! Joseph Smith was present in Kirtland that Easter Sunday in 1836 to witness the glorious appearance of Elijah and receive from his hands the sealing keys of the holy priesthood. As Joseph's understanding of the significance of that event deepened—or, perhaps more appropriately, *heightened*—as he envisioned its meaning for all the living and the dead, he joyfully exclaimed:

> Brethren, shall we not go on in so great a cause? Go forward and not backward. Courage, brethren; and on, on to the victory! Let your hearts rejoice, and be exceedingly glad. Let the earth break forth into singing. Let the dead speak forth anthems of eternal praise to the King Immanuel, who hath ordained, before the world was, that which would enable us to redeem them out of their prison; for the prisoners shall go free.
>
> Let the mountains shout for joy, and all ye valleys cry aloud; and all ye seas and dry lands tell the wonders of your Eternal King! And ye rivers, and brooks, and rills, flow down with gladness. Let the woods and all the trees of the field praise the Lord; and ye solid rocks weep for joy! And let the sun, moon, and the morning stars sing together, and let all the sons of God shout for joy! And let the eternal

creations declare his name forever and ever! And again I say, how glorious is the voice we hear from heaven, proclaiming in our ears, glory, and salvation, and honor, and immortality, and eternal life; kingdoms, principalities, and powers! (D&C 128:22–23.)

Elijah, our thoughts turn again to you. We are overwhelmed with gratitude for the lessons we have learned from studying the example of your life, faith, and obedience. We wish to thank you for helping us remember the importance of the new and everlasting covenant, and for helping to engrave that covenant upon our hearts. Thank you for restoring the sealing keys of the holy priesthood to make permanent and eternal the ordinances that bind us to those we love. Thank you for helping guide us back to the One who gave you this assignment and this power, the Lord Jehovah himself. You came to prepare us for his second coming. Being filled with love and the glorious vision of this work, we thank you, Elijah. By our lives of love, service, and obedience, may we each demonstrate that *our* hearts have turned, so that we will be ready for that approaching great and dreadful day. Looking forward with joy and anticipation, may we echo the final prayer of the beloved disciple John, "Even so, come, Lord Jesus" (Revelation 22:20).

Appendix A

JEWISH TRADITIONS ABOUT THE HISTORICAL ELIJAH

THIS APPENDIX CONTAINS JEWISH traditions that expound on the events surrounding the biblical or historical record of Elijah's life. These traditions span a broad range of subjects and explain everything from Elijah's appearance to his translation. The material presented here conveys the traditional context of Elijah's earthly ministry and provides us with some creative possibilities to fill in the textual gaps in the biblical narrative.

Jewish traditions about Elijah often speculate about his personal life and even his appearance. Many sources insist that Elijah never married and had no children. They give different reasons for this, but most agree that Elijah needed to be free from anything that might deviate or distract him from his prophetic responsibilities.[1] According to some tales, people scoffed at Elijah for his appearance, saying that he was an "ugly" man.[2] Supposedly both his odd hairstyle and his unusually large amount of body hair provoked the mockery of the people.[3]

Despite the challenges that he might have faced, Elijah was a prophet who possessed divinely delegated authority, as evidenced by his sealing of the heavens. When famine covered the land, Elijah migrated to the brook Cherith, where there was an ample supply of fresh water and an abundance of food that ravens brought from the kitchen of the righteous King Jehoshaphat in Jerusalem. Another tradition states that the food given to Elijah by the ravens was his priestly portion brought from the temple in Jerusalem.[4] When God felt that the famine had adequately humbled the Israelites, he gently encouraged Elijah to revoke his curse by drying up the brook that had sustained Elijah's life.[5]

Instead of succumbing to God's encouragement, Elijah is said to have simply moved his residence—this time to Zarephath in search of a new supply of food and water. Luckily, the prophet found a willing widow that was prepared to give all she had to this newcomer. Unexpectedly, the widow's son died, an event that devastated the widow and baffled Elijah. The widow, searching for an explanation for this tragic event, asked Elijah, "What have I to do with thee, O thou man of God? art thou come unto me to call my sin to remembrance, and to slay my son?" (1 Kings 17:18.) Elijah pleaded with the Lord to restore life to the boy, but God reminded Elijah that resuscitation could be done only by using fresh morning dew, and as a result of the drought, there was no moisture at all, not even dew.[6] Elijah, realizing that he was cornered, knew that he would have to bargain with God. The Lord had given Elijah the "key of rain," but had kept for himself the "key of birth" and the "key of the quickening of the dead." So when Elijah asked for the "key of the quickening of the dead," God told him that it was not appropriate that Elijah, being the servant, have two of the three keys. Elijah thus agreed to trade the "key of rain" for the "key of the quickening of the dead,"[7] and used this power to restore the boy's life. Some traditions indicate that this boy later became the prophet Jonah.[8]

With the coming end of the drought, the Lord sent Elijah to confront the priests of Baal on Mount Carmel (see 1 Kings 18:1–20). The contest that Elijah arranged required two young bulls to be sacrificed—one upon the altar dedicated to Jehovah and the other upon the altar dedicated to Baal. When a pair of twin bulls was found to supply this need, Elijah easily led his bull up to the altar, but all the priests of Baal together could not make their bull budge. Elijah approached the bull to see what the prob-lem was, and the bull opened his mouth, saying, "We two, yonder bullock and myself, came forth from the same womb, we took our food from the same manger, and now he has been destined for God, as an instrument for the glorification of the Divine Name, while I am to be used for Baal, as an instrument to enrage my Creator." Elijah assured the bull that his glory would be no less than that of his twin, and thus the bull allowed Elijah to lead him to the altar of the priests of Baal.[9]

During the course of the contest, the idolatrous priests realized that their cause was for naught, so rather than admit defeat they thought they could deceive the people by digging a trench under-neath their altar so that a man could hide and ignite the sacrifice at the appointed time. The man assigned to hide under the altar was Hiel, the same who rebuilt Jericho (see 1 Kings 16:34). God ended this mischievousness by sending a poisonous serpent to kill Hiel as he hid beneath the altar.[10]

By the time the priests of Baal had made their vain attempt to call down heavenly fire to consume their sacrifice, it was late in the day and Elijah had little time to prepare and offer his sacrifice. This, however, was not a problem, as Elijah simply commanded the sun to stand still: "For Joshua thou didst stand still that Israel might conquer his enemies; now stand thou still, neither for my sake, nor for the sake of Israel, but that the name of God may be exalted."[11] With the setting of the sun halted, Elijah could now make the final preparations for his sacrifice to God.

Elisha, associated with the servant mentioned in 1 Kings 18:43, helped Elijah drench the sacrifice with water from barrels, but that was not enough to adequately wet the sacrifice—they needed another source of water. Elijah instructed Elisha to pour a small amount of water over Elijah's hands, after which ten springs of water gushed forth from the prophet's fingers, which thoroughly soaked the sacrifice.[12]

Following the fiery consumption of the sacrifice and the subse-quent slaying of the priests of Baal (see 1 Kings 18:40), Elijah "cast himself down upon the earth, and put his face between his knees"

(1 Kings 18:42). Traditions suggest that he did this as he besought God to remember the covenant that he had made with Israel, the sign or token of which was circumcision. By looking "between his knees," Elijah viewed the part of the body bearing the sign of the covenant.[13] As Elijah invoked God to remember the covenant, he also pleaded for the righteousness of past generations, known as the "merits of the fathers," to make up for the failings of the current generation.[14] The prayers of Elijah were answered with the rain that subsequently poured out upon the land.[15] Jewish legend reports that this rain symbolized God's remembrance of the covenant and his forgiveness of the people.

Elijah had hoped that the convincing demonstration on Mount Carmel would change the hearts of Ahab and Jezebel. To Elijah's dismay, the monarchy only became more hardened and even sought his life. Thus, he fled to Horeb. In his exhaustive work *The Legends of the Jews*, Louis Ginzberg remarks, "In the cleft of the rock in which God had once aforetimes appeared to Moses, and revealed Himself as compassionate and long-suffering, He now met with Elijah."[16] Some sources claim that this cave was also the one in which God buried Moses.[17] The reason that this cave was so special was that it was created at twilight on the sixth day of the Creation, just before the onset of the Sabbath.[18]

While on Horeb, Elijah had a life-changing encounter with a great wind, earthquake, fire, and, ultimately, the still small voice. Many legends surround the interpretation of these fantastic events. One version says that this experience was a vision meant to instruct Elijah concerning the destiny of man. The wind represented the world, which is as fleeting as the wind. The earthquake symbolized the "day of death" that makes the human body tremble and quake. Fire was the judgement day in Gehenna (hell), and the stillness of the last day was portrayed by the still small voice.[19] Another tradition states that this was a revelation concerning the three classes of angels ("angels of wind," "angels of storm," and "angels of fire") and that God then revealed himself to Elijah as the still small voice.[20]

At the end of his mortal ministry, Elijah was taken up by a "chariot of fire," according to the biblical account. Nevertheless there was apparently one previous attempt to retire Elijah from mortality. God sent an angel to invite Elijah to return to heaven, but when the angel arrived on the scene, he found Elijah and Elisha so intensely engaged in a scholarly conversation that he could not get their attention and had to return empty-handed.[21]

Jewish Traditions About Elijah as a Healer and Helper

Even beyond his importance as a mortal prophet, traditions recount that Elijah continued to serve in numerous ways after his translation. Among the services he rendered were those of medical healer and general helper. In the medical arena, Elijah administered a remedy to a serpent-swallowing rabbi, and he healed a toothache by the "laying on of hands." Furthermore, Elijah protected the Jewish people from poverty, the angel of death, cruel rulers, and scheming thieves. Because of his unparalleled service, Elijah is "remembered to be good."

As a healer, Elijah assisted many people as a divinely sent doctor who cured people of a wide variety of infirmities and ailments. In one instance, a prominent man, Rabbi Shimi Bar Ashi, swallowed a snake, which obviously caused him significant difficulty. Elijah appeared as a horseman in this moment of despair and immediately administered a remedy that consisted of eating a medicinal herb and running approximately two miles. This cure caused the rabbi to vomit, ridding himself of the serpent.[1] Rabbi Judah ha-Nasi was another who was healed at the hand of Elijah. Rabbi Judah had suffered from a toothache for forty years and found absolutely no relief in any remedy he tried. Elijah, noting the distress of the good rabbi, came to him in the form of another rabbi, laid his hands on Rabbi Judah, and cured him of his toothache.[2]

Elijah acted as a helper to the Jewish people in many different ways. Sometimes he resorted to rather drastic measures to help someone in need. For instance, on one occasion Elijah gave himself as a slave to a poor man so that the poor man could sell him and receive the profits. The man did as Elijah said and sold the prophet to a wealthy prince for a large sum of money, making himself rich for the rest of his life. Shortly thereafter, the prince decided to build a palace and he began searching for an architect to design and build it. Elijah ended the search by offering his abilities as an architect and contractor. The prince agreed to his proposal and promised Elijah his freedom if he could finish building the palace within six months. Elijah surprised the prince and gained his freedom when the palace was beautifully completed the very next morning.[3]

In addition to rescuing select individuals from poverty, Elijah has helped the Jewish people with things such as fertility, child bearing, and protecting children from the angel of death. He searches for opportunities to serve as he walks the streets disguised as a beggar[4]—the barking of dogs is a sure sign that he is in the neighborhood.[5] For these reasons, the Jews say that Elijah is always "remembered to be good."[6]

Elijah was often "remembered to be good" because of the help he rendered during political crises—on several occasions he appeared to and changed the hearts of cruel rulers who persecuted the Jews. One example of this involved Elijah's appearance to the calif Al-Mutadhid. The calif regularly tormented the Jews until Elijah visited him in a dream and threatened him with a torturous death if he did not change his attitude toward the Jews.[7] Sultan Sulaiman I of the Ottoman Empire reportedly had a similar experience that halted his poor treatment of the Jews. Sulaiman had decided to start a particularly cruel campaign against the Jews but was abruptly stopped by Elijah. Sulaiman remained so impressed by the experience that he became a staunch friend of the Jewish community. For this change of heart, Elijah rewarded Sulaiman with a personal visitation every month.[8]

Elijah also helped Nahum of Gimzo avert a crisis when Nahum journeyed to Rome as an emissary on behalf of the Jews. Wanting to impress the emperor, Nahum brought gems and treasures to give to the monarch. En route, however, a group of thieves secretly stole the treasury and replaced it with dirt. When Nahum arrived in Rome, he opened the chest to present the treasure to the emperor, but found dirt instead of diamonds. Certain that Nahum and the entire Jewish nation were mocking him, the Roman emperor sentenced Nahum to death. Elijah, sensing the urgency of the situation, appeared as a court official and told the emperor that this was not just any ordinary dirt but it was the "dirt of Abraham," and whoever carried it into battle and sprinkled it on the land could not be defeated. The emperor's men experimented with the dirt and found Elijah's claim to be true. Impressed with the gift, the ruler released Nahum and showered his company with riches, praise, and honor.[9]

JEWISH TRADITIONS ABOUT ELIJAH AS A TEACHER AND REVELATOR

AS PART OF HIS RESPONSIBILITIES TO HELP mankind, Elijah is reported to have taken it upon himself to train and instruct mortals. His experiences in this capacity range from the teaching of simple moral stories to the revelation of profound celestial secrets. For instance, he taught lessons about humility and revealed the power that can be unlocked by the prayers of the righteous. Through this tutelage many great men and women were molded, enlightened, and brought nearer to their God. In this sense, Elijah served as a teacher and revelator.

As a teacher, Elijah retained much of the strictness and zeal that had won him fame in Old Testament times. Furthermore, his campaign against idolatry continued as he worked to keep the Jews free from its taint. Elijah was very strict with his associates—any wrong move on their part could result in the alienation of Elijah and the cessation of his visits.[1] One rabbi commented that Elijah was "passionate and irascible."[2]

Elijah's zealousness was generated by his devotion to Deity as seen in the following legend. After the destruction of Jerusalem by

Rome in A.D. 70, Elijah walked the rubble-strewn streets in an attempt to ascertain whether the people had deserved this calamity. He came across one little boy who was alone, lying on a dungheap, and promised the youth that he would live if he merely recited the words of the "Shema." (The Shema is a Jewish prayer recited in the morning and evening and at night just before going to bed. It is considered important because it declares the monotheism of God and refutes idolatry.[3]) However, as Elijah began reciting the Shema, the youth refused to participate and subsequently died hugging and kissing his idols.[4]

Elijah, as the tutor of numerous rabbis, was very interested in helping them understand the importance of humility and the cankering effects of pride. He taught one of the rabbis an important lesson one day as they walked past a decayed carcass that smelled terrible. The rabbi, gagging from the putrid smell, plugged his nose until they passed, but noticed that Elijah remained unaffected. A short time later, the pair walked past a proud and haughty man; this time Elijah plugged his nose—an action that perplexed the rabbi. Elijah later explained: "The proud man is worse than the carcass; if one touches a carcass, he becomes defiled only until sunset; but contact with the proud generates impurities lasting for a long time."[5]

As a teacher of heavenly truths, Elijah revealed attributes that would enable one to secure a place in the world to come. He taught this lesson to Rabbi Joshua ben Levi as they entered a crowded marketplace and the rabbi asked Elijah who would have a place in the heavenly realm. Elijah at first responded that none of those whom he saw would have a place in the world to come, but he then changed his mind upon spotting two jesters and a jail warden. He explained that the jail warden would have a place there because he preserved the chastity of the men and women inmates. The two jesters would also find a place in the world to come because they made it their daily activity to lighten the mental burdens of the people by telling jokes and making them laugh.[6]

We see one of the greatest demonstrations of Elijah's power as a teacher in another experience he had with Rabbi Joshua ben Levi. Because of the rabbi's faithfulness, Elijah granted him any wish he desired. Rabbi Joshua explained to Elijah that the only thing he really wanted was to accompany Elijah on his travels throughout the world. After pondering the proposal, Elijah consented but stipulated that the rabbi must never question his actions. If he did they would have to part ways. As they traveled, they first came upon an elderly couple who possessed little more than a cow. As Elijah and the rabbi passed the couple, the rabbi noticed that Elijah was praying that the cow would die. This greatly confused Rabbi Joshua, but he said nothing at the moment. The next stop was at the home of a wealthy but very proud and inconsiderate man. Much to Rabbi Joshua's surprise, Elijah magically rebuilt a broken wall in the man's expansive house. They then came upon a faithful congregation of pious believers that received them with tremendous hospitality. The rabbi again found it odd that Elijah prayed that the congregation would produce but one leader. The next congregation they encountered was just the opposite of the first; it consisted of proud and arrogant men and women who treated Elijah and the rabbi with very little respect. This time Elijah prayed that the congregation would have many leaders.

At this point Rabbi Joshua could no longer contain his bewilderment. Elijah agreed to explain why he had acted in each situation as he had. In the first case, Elijah prayed that God would allow the man's cow to die rather than his wife, for she was on the brink of death. When they came to the house of the rich man, Elijah prayed that the wall would be rebuilt so that the rich man would not find the treasure buried beneath it. The first congregation was blessed to have only one leader because a congregation having only one leader will enjoy peace and harmony. He blessed the second congregation to have many leaders, which would cause strife and division among the people. Thus, Elijah's blessings were in a sense cursings, and the apparent cursings were truly blessings.[7]

Even though he was zealous in his teaching, Elijah was wise enough to let men choose for themselves and then face the consequences of their decisions. For example, Rabbi Joseph della Rosa sincerely believed that he could redeem man by defeating the angel of death. Elijah counseled him on many occasions that this was not a wise approach to the redemption of man, but Rabbi Joseph was so persistent that Elijah agreed to tutor him in the tactics and strategies he would need in order to defeat the angel of death. Despite all the training and tutoring, when Rabbi della Rosa finally faced the angel of death, he made a fatal mistake that cost him his life.[8]

As part of being a teacher, Elijah revealed sacred truths to those whom he deemed worthy. When he felt that he could not provide adequate answers, he was even willing to refer diligent disciples to a higher source. On one occasion he arranged for an interview between the Messiah and Rabbi Joshua ben Levi. At the time of the interview, Elijah also showed Rabbi Joshua a pair of "precious stones" that were so bright that they would replace the sun in giving light to Jerusalem during the messianic time.[9]

One tradition recounts the time when Elijah revealed too much about celestial events. On one of Elijah's daily visits to the academy of Rabbi Judah ha-Nasi, he arrived late, explaining that the delay arose from some complications in the waking of the three patriarchs Abraham, Isaac, and Jacob for their daily prayers. The task was rather time-consuming, since Elijah had to prepare each patriarch individually and at a separate time to offer up his prayers. They prayed at different times because if they prayed together, their petition would be so strong that God would be forced to send the Messiah before the appropriate time for his coming. Rabbi Judah listened intently to Elijah's explanation and, seeing an opportunity, asked Elijah if there were any three people on earth that could combine their prayers in such a way that the effect would be the same as the combined prayers of the patriarchs. Elijah confirmed that there were three such people and identified them as Rabbi Hayyah and his two sons. Rabbi Judah wasted no time in gathering Rabbi Hayyah and his two sons for a day of fasting and prayer. Their combined prayer was so powerful that when they mentioned "wind" a great storm arose. Rain also instantly fell when they prayed for it. When Elijah and the rest of the heavenly host realized that disaster was impending, Elijah appeared in the form of a she-bear and broke up the praying congregation.[10]

Appendix D

JEWISH TRADITIONS ABOUT ELIJAH IN THE HEAVENLY REALM

THE MANY TRADITIONS CONCERNING the prophet Elijah extend beyond his earthly sojourn into the heavenly realm, indicating that Elijah did specific things in the postmortal world. In the heavenly realm, Elijah continues to minister to the condemned souls in Gehenna (hell), and he acts as a scribe in recording the deeds of all mankind. Getting into the heavenly realm at the end of his mortal existence was not easy, however. He had to first confront the angel of death.

As we have seen, the biblical account of Elijah's ministry abruptly ends in 2 Kings 2 with his ascension to heaven in a chariot of fire. Many traditions pick up where the Bible leaves off, specifying that upon arriving at the gates of heaven, the angel of death, also known as Sammael,[1] refused to allow Elijah to enter heaven. At the Creation, however, God had specifically told Sammael to let Elijah enter heaven when he was translated. The only way to appease both sides was to arrange a physical contest between Elijah and Sammael. Elijah, having won the contest, was on the brink of utterly destroying Sammael when God restrained him. With the angel of death underfoot, Elijah ascended to his heavenly abode.[2] Another account reveals that it was not his defeat of Sammael that allowed him to enter but rather his giving of specific "Holy Names" needed to enter. Yet another legend claims that Sammael actually helped Elijah get into heaven by giving him a remedy for death that would also enable him to be translated.[3]

Despite his translation and victory over the angel of death, the majority of these sources agree that Elijah did not enter heaven proper. Most say that Elijah and his fellow prophet Moses dwell in close vicinity to heaven, but not in heaven itself. This is complicated by the uncertainty of the location of paradise. Many claim that paradise and heaven are two separate entities and that Elijah and Moses, while dwelling in paradise, do not frequent the grounds of heaven proper.[4]

Some legends of Elijah that pertain to the celestial sphere reveal many of his characteristics. Some traditions refer to him as the "tall angel," purporting that he is one of the tallest angels in the celestial realm.[5] He also holds the title of "master of heavenly song." He generally wears sandals when in the presence of the Maker,[6] and he is known as one of the greatest and mightiest of the fiery angelic host,[7] being counted as one of the great *sarim*, or "angelic princes."[8] Elijah, as a prominent heavenly personality, is considered to be in the same category as the Messiah ben David, the Messiah ben Joseph, and Melchizedek.[9]

One of Elijah's primary duties as a leader in the heavenly realm is to guide the deceased inhabitants of the earth to their final destinations in heaven. Standing at the crossroads of the "road of justice," which leads to Gehenna, and the "road of love," which leads to heaven, Elijah directs the righteous to the "road of love" and sends the wicked along the "road of justice."[10] Despite the fact that Elijah must send some to Gehenna, he continues to care about them. At the beginning of the Sabbath each week, Elijah leads the damned souls out of Gehenna and proceeds to teach and train them. When the wicked have finally atoned for their sins, Elijah releases them from their torment in Gehenna and leads them to paradise.[11]

Another duty of Elijah is that of scribe for the human race. As a heavenly scribe, he works with Enoch in recording the daily deeds of mankind.[12] He sits beneath the tree of life as he makes his record—he pays particular attention to recording the deeds of those who observe the Sabbath.[13] Elijah records these deeds on the skins of animals that he has sacrificed to make atonement for the children of Israel.[14]

Appendix E

JEWISH TRADITIONS ABOUT ELIJAH AS A DEFENDER OF THE COVENANT AND THE FAMILY

AMONG THE SPOOLS OF ELIJAH LORE, we encounter occasional threads that deal with topics that are of special interest to Latter-day Saints. Two aspects of Elijah lore that fit into this category proclaim Elijah as the defender of the covenant and the family. In the Jewish legends, we find Elijah sanctioning circumcisions (the token of the covenant), recording marriages, and revealing genealogies. This he does as the "messenger of the covenant" that Malachi prophesied would "turn the heart of the fathers to the children, and the heart of the children to their fathers" (Malachi 4:6).

Elijah is often called the "messenger of the covenant"[1] or the "angel of the covenant"[2] in connection with the prophecies found in Malachi 3:1 and 4:5–6 regarding his return. Numerous traditions connect his responsibility of maintaining the covenant with the zeal that he demonstrated in his encounter with the Israelite monarchy and the priests of Baal. Because of his tireless efforts in fighting idolatry, God gave Elijah the charge of making sure that Israel keeps its covenants.[3] Given that the token of the covenant is circumcision, Elijah is naturally involved in ceremonial circumcisions. Many legends report that Elijah was assigned to be present at *every* circumcision, albeit invisibly, to verify the keeping of the covenant.[4] Due to Elijah's connection with circumcision, the Jews use a heavily ornamented chair known as the "Chair of Elijah" upon which they perform circumcision.[5]

One particular story demonstrates the importance of Elijah's approval of the circumcision ceremony. During one such event, the presiding rabbi remained very silent. When asked why he refused to speak, the rabbi responded that he did not see Elijah seated at his side. The rabbi then stood up and went to the window to talk with an old man standing outside, who was none other than Elijah. Elijah told the rabbi that he refused to be present at the circumcision ceremony because the young boy who was being circumcised would one day abandon Judaism. The prophecy was fulfilled when the boy grew to manhood and forsook the faith of his fathers.[6]

One of the most important duties belonging to the prophet Elijah is that of keeping and protecting families, both in this world and in the world to come. The Jews have many legends that refer to Elijah's involvement in the preservation of families, which he does by virtue of the power and responsibility given to him by God. Many legends recount that when Elijah returns to the earth, he will make peace among the nations, reassemble families, and designate who are genuine Israelites.[7] He will resolve any questions of genealogy and will make known *all* genealogies.[8]

Elijah also zealously guards the ritual purity of families. Marriages are of utmost importance, and it has been written among the traditions of the Jews that "he who marries a woman worthy of him is loved by God and kissed by Elijah; but he who marries an unworthy woman is hated by God and flogged by Elijah."[9] We read elsewhere, "Every marriage is recorded in writing by Elijah and God affixes His seal to the marriage record."[10] Elijah protects the children produced by these marriages by helping them and their mothers through the trauma of childbirth and acting as their guardian against witches.[11] Louis Ginzberg summarizes Elijah's role in the following manner, "Elijah will restore peace and harmony in Israel. All these views presuppose that Elijah's chief activity will consist in restoring the purity of the family."[12]

Appendix F

JEWISH TRADITIONS ABOUT ELIJAH AND THE PASSOVER

THE JEWISH PASSOVER ANNUALLY celebrates the night in ancient Egypt when the angel of death "passed over" the children of Israel, sparing them from the destruction that overtook the first-born of all Egyptian families. Elijah's association with Passover festivities most likely stems from his association with the messianic age. Elijah, according to Jewish belief, will be the forerunner of the Messiah. In preparation for the Messiah's coming, he will resolve doubts and restore peace to the earth. He is significant in the Passover because the Passover not only is a celebration of past deliverance but also looks to future freedom from bondage. As the Jewish people look to Elijah for the resolution of doubts and as a bearer of peace, his ministry has become intimately intertwined with the Passover feast.

Following the recitation of the part of the Passover service known as the "Grace After Meals," the Passover participants fill Elijah's cup with wine and place it at the center of the table.[1] They reserve a special chair for the expected guest,[2] and upon the

opening of the door, all present stand and greet the prophet with
the words:

> O pour out Thy wrath upon the nations that know Thee not, and
> upon the kingdoms that call not upon Thy name. For they have de-
> voured Jacob, and laid waste his land. Pour out Thy indignation
> upon them, and let the fierceness of Thy anger overtake them.
> Pursue them in anger, and destroy them from under the heavens of
> the Lord.[3]

In the context of the Passover, the door that is opened for
Elijah takes on special significance. The house's east-facing door is
the preferred door through which the family invites Elijah to enter
the house. Tradition predicts that in the last day, the Messiah will
come from the east. It is therefore natural to assume that the forerunner of the Messiah, Elijah, will also come from the east.
Symbolically, then, the eastern doors of the homes of observant
Jews throughout the world are opened at the Passover to invite the
coming of Elijah preparatory to the awaited opening of the East
Gate of Jerusalem to welcome the Messiah.[4]

A child is sent to open the door for Elijah because children
represent the hope and promise of the future. In this respect, the
child's opening the door metaphorically represents the hope and
promise associated with the coming of Elijah.[5] When the door is
closed, all are seated[6] and the children hurriedly move toward the
table to meticulously check the level of the wine to see whether
Elijah has sipped from his cup.[7]

While the tradition of opening the door for Elijah extends
back to Talmudic times, the tradition of Elijah's cup is a relatively
new addition to the Passover celebration. During earlier centuries,
Elijah apparently played a limited role in the traditions and festivities surrounding Passover. Then, however, in the eighteenth century A.D.[8] there arose a dispute about how many glasses of wine
should be drunk at the Passover feast. Based on Exodus 6:6–7,
many of the scholars said that four glasses of wine should be drunk:
"Wherefore say unto the children of Israel, I am the Lord, and *I
will bring you out* from under the burdens of the Egyptians, and *I*

will rid you out of their bondage, and *I will redeem you* with a stretched out arm, and with great judgments: and *I will take you* to me for a people, and I will be to you a God: and ye shall know that I am the Lord your God, which bringeth you out from under the burdens of the Egyptians." (Italics added.) Each of the four glasses of wine represents one of the promises included in these verses: "I will bring you out," "I will rid you out of their bondage," "I will redeem you," and "I will take you."[9] The opposing school of thought reasoned that while these four phrases must definitely be represented with cups of wine, there is also a fifth one that should be recognized with wine: "And *I will bring you in unto the land,* concerning the which I did swear to give it to Abraham, to Isaac, and to Jacob; and I will give it you for an heritage: I am the Lord" (Exodus 6:8; italics added). The phrase, "I will bring you in unto the land" was the phrase upon which they based this argument. After much examination of this doctrinal dilemma, the rabbis agreed that because Elijah will resolve all doubts and religious questions, the fifth and final cup of wine should be reserved for him. This undrunk cup came to be known as the "cup of Elijah."[10]

Through these ritual traditions—the opening of the door for Elijah, the reservation of a seat for him, and the presence of his cup—linked with the Passover feast, we see the profound degree to which the Jewish soul remembers and respects Elijah. With every year and every Passover feast, the Jews are reminded that the man who in millennia past saved them from spiritual harm continues to succor them through the trials of the present.

Appendix G

JEWISH LEGENDS
ABOUT ELIJAH AS THE
FORERUNNER OF THE MESSIAH
AND RESTORER

ELIJAH, ACCORDING TO JEWISH LORE, WILL be the forerunner of the Messiah and will usher in the messianic age in the last days. He will reveal truth and resolve doubts as he prepares the Jewish people for the coming of the Messiah, after which Elijah will introduce the Messiah to the house of Israel. At the end of time, he will also "turn the heart of the fathers to the children, and the heart of the children to their fathers," and banish evil forever.

Elijah is often referred to as the "herald" of the messianic era who will "make the truth known."[1] The Jews look to the coming of Elijah with the hope of having difficult ethical, legal, religious, and moral issues resolved,[2] for "all differences of opinion must be removed from the path of the Messiah"[3] before he comes. Frequent phrases in Jewish literature represent this belief about Elijah's role, such as "This must remain undecided until Elijah comes,"[4] and "This passage will be interpreted by Elijah in the future."[5] Not surprisingly, one of Elijah's many tasks during the messianic age will be to interpret the law.[6]

Jewish legends report that the messianic era will begin during the Passover season, and Elijah's public preparation for the coming of the Messiah will begin three days before the Messiah's appearance. On the first day, Elijah will go to the Holy Land and weep over the destruction that has taken place there.[7] So loud will be his weeping that it will be heard throughout the world. Following his lament, Elijah will proclaim, "Now peace will come upon the earth!" On the second day, Elijah will say, "Good will come upon earth!" He will then promise on the third day of preparation that "salvation will come upon earth!" Following this third proclamation, Michael will blow his *shofar* (a ram's horn that makes a trumpet-like sound) and Elijah will come forth to introduce the Messiah. The people observing these events will then request that the Messiah resurrect many people to prove that he is indeed the true Messiah.[8]

After resurrecting many of the dead, the Messiah will work seven miracles: (1) he will bring Moses and the desert generation of the Exodus back to life; (2) he will raise Korah and his group (see Numbers 16:1–35) from out of the earth; (3) he will resurrect the Messiah ben Joseph, who was slain; (4) he will show the three holy vessels of the temple—the ark of the covenant, the flask of manna, and the cruse of sacred oil—that mysteriously disappeared;[9] (5) he will wave the scepter given to him by God; (6) he will level the mountains of the Holy Land; and (7) he will reveal the "great mystery," or the secret of redemption. "Then the Jews will believe that Elijah is the Elijah promised to them, and the Messiah introduced by him is the true Messiah."[10]

On that last great day of redemption, the promise given by Malachi concerning Elijah (see Malachi 4:5–6) will be fulfilled— the hearts of the children will be turned to their fathers. The children who died as a result of the sins of their fathers will all be saved in paradise; their wicked fathers, however, will be found on the other side of the chasm, suffering eternal torment in Gehenna. These children, seeing their fathers suffer, will beg them to come to them, but God will not allow it, so Elijah will teach the children how to pray on behalf of their wicked fathers. God will answer the prayers of the children by allowing the fathers to leave Gehenna and go to their children in paradise. In this manner the hearts of the children will be turned to their fathers.[11]

One of the last and most important events of Elijah's illustrious career will be the slaying of Sammael, the angel of death, at God's command. This act will banish evil forever.[12] With the peace of the messianic reign in place, eight princes—Elijah, Jesse, Saul, Samuel, Amos, Zephaniah, Zedekiah, and the Messiah—will form the administrative body governing the earth.[13]

ELIJAH IN
CHRISTIAN TRADITION

ONE OF THE DIFFICULTIES OF WRITING a section devoted to
Christian traditions about the prophet Elijah is that historically,
and often doctrinally, Christianity and Judaism are tightly intertwined. Nevertheless, the Christians possess many of their own
traditions that explain everything from Elijah's personal life to his
final battle with the anti-Christ. Predictably, there are events from
Elijah's life that are overlaid with Christian theology. For instance,
some believe that Elijah saw a vision of the Virgin Mary. Like the
Jewish legends, however, these Christian traditions serve to em-
phasize Elijah's tremendous importance in the beliefs of many.

The Christians, like the Jews, have their own legends about
Elijah's origin, personal life, and ministry. Christian lore states that
Elijah was a Tishbite from the land of the Arabs and that following
his birth angels swaddled him in fire, gave him a flame to eat, and
announced to Elijah's father, Sabacha, that Elijah would one day
judge Israel.[1] Christian literature honors Elijah not only because
he was a great prophet but also because he was a celibate[2] and a
virgin.[3] Many Christians also subscribe to the idea that the son of
the widow of Zarephath whom Elijah brought back to life grew up

to become the prophet Jonah.[4] Elijah's forty-day fast is often compared to the fasts of Moses and Christ, and Christian tradition confirms that Elijah went to the cave on Mount Sinai (Horeb) where Moses met God in the burning bush. This cave, according to the early Christian fathers, lies only three miles from the present-day location of St. Catherine's monastery at the base of Mount Sinai.[5] In the Christian era, legends maintain that Moses and Elijah were the two angels that appeared at Jesus' tomb. The early Christian fathers further claimed that they received Elijah's sealing power and were thus the rightful heirs in the prophetic line.[6]

There is a whole subset of Christian legends that come from the Carmelites, a monastic order founded on Mount Carmel—the region where Elijah defeated the priests of Baal. These monks trace the origins of their order back to Elijah, viewing him as the order's founder,[7] and they claim that Elijah and his successor, Elisha, started a school of prophets around 700 B.C.[8] This order became officially Catholic by order of the popes of the twelfth and thirteenth centuries A.D. Due to Elijah's isolated lifestyle, some have called him the "first monk."[9] The Carmelites consider Elijah to be preeminent among the prophets because he represented all the prophets who preceded him when he appeared before Jesus Christ on the Mount of Transfiguration. Gabriel's proclamation that John the Baptist would come "in the spirit and power of Elias"[10] also manifests his importance, as does the Carmelite belief that Elijah's translation reserved him for the final battle between good and evil that will occur in the last day.[11]

The Carmelites say Elijah dwelt on Mount Carmel for most of his adult life and thus was very familiar with the area in which he would perform miracles and confront idolatry.[12] Their tradition states that after slaying the priests of Baal, Elijah went to the top of the mountain to look for clouds in the west, searching for the sign of rain that would end the three years of drought. Accompanying the small cloud that he saw forming over the Mediterranean Elijah saw a vision of the Virgin Mary rising out of the sea, inspiring him to found the religious order that would eventually evolve into the modern Carmelites.[13]

The translation of Elijah seems to be very important in the traditions of groups that have any connection with him. Not surprisingly, many of the early Christian writers agreed with their Jewish counterparts that Elijah was translated to a different sphere, but not directly to heaven itself. St. Augustine discussed and clarified Elijah's current status, saying that the prophet "now possesses something better than he could have had in this life, but he does not yet have what he is to possess on the last day as a reward for his life of faithful service." The general feeling among the early Christian writers was that translation was a transitional state rather than a final one.[14]

Malachi's prophecy of Elijah's return generated many rumors about when he would come and what he would do. The Christian answers to such questions are believed to be found in the New Testament personage of John. John seemingly denied that he was "Elias" (the Greek form of the name "Elijah"), and yet Christ later linked John the Baptist and Elijah in the following statement: "And Jesus answered and said unto them, Elias truly shall first come, and restore all things. But I say unto you, That Elias is come already, and they knew him not, but have done unto him whatsoever they listed. Likewise shall also the Son of man suffer of them. Then the disciples understood that he spake unto them of John the Baptist." (Matthew 17:11–13.)

Some modern Christian scholars tend to believe that John the Baptist was indeed Elijah, and that there is no need to look for any future coming of the prophet.[15] It is interesting, however, that many of the early Christian writers alluded to the fact that John the Baptist and Elijah were not the same person.[16] St. Augustine, writing in the fifth century A.D., explained: "As there are two comings of the Judge, there will be two heralds. The [Judge] sent before Him the first herald [John] calling him Elia, because Elia would be in the Second Coming what John was in the first."[17] This remark seems to indicate that the scholars who lived closer to Christ's lifetime believed that John and Elijah were separate beings and that Elijah would be the one to prepare the way for the coming of Christ in the last days.

According to legend, Elijah and Enoch will serve a special
mission in the last days in which they will be killed by the anti-
Christ and will then be resurrected three days later. One source
states that Elijah and Enoch will be put to death on an altar by the
anti-Christ and then will be raised again by two angels who are
identified as Michael and Gabriel and will thus be able to continue the fight against the anti-Christ.[18] It has been rumored that
the anti-Christ will come from the tribe of Dan,[19] probably because Dan is not listed with the other tribes in Revelation 7:5–8.
After Elijah and Enoch have killed the anti-Christ and banished
evil forever,[20] Elijah will ceremoniously anoint Christ, the long-
awaited Messiah.[21]

As part of the preparation for the coming of Christ, Malachi's
prophecy of the turning of hearts will be fulfilled. According to
Christian lore, turning the hearts of the fathers to children and
vice versa refers to the conversion of the Jews in the latter days.[22]
The synagogues will be turned towards Christ and they will accept
him as their Messiah.[23] St. Augustine wrote extensively on the
conversion of the Jews at the coming of Christ, indicating they
would first see the love that God has for Christ, whom they had
previously rejected. This new understanding of Christ and his relationship to the Father would enable them to truly understand the
law as practiced by Moses and the other prophets of old. Thus they
would turn their hearts toward their fathers, the prophets of old,
for greater understanding of the law and of God's plan. When the
ancient prophets see that the modern Jews have finally come out
of apostasy, their hearts will be turned to them and all will be rec-
onciled.[24]

Appendix I

ISLAMIC LORE
ABOUT ELIJAH

ISLAMIC TRADITIONS ABOUT THE PROPHET Elijah are not as abundant as their Jewish or Christian counterparts, but they still form an important part of the Elijah lore found in the major world religions. The Islamic versions of Elijah legends are, in many instances, repeats of Jewish traditions retold with an Islamic twist. For instance, Islamic lore explains Elijah's origin and details of his ministry in ways that are similar to previously seen Jewish accounts. These legends, nonetheless, confirm the importance and prominence of Elijah in Islam.

The Koran, the holy book of Islam, refers to Elijah by the Greek rendition of his name, "Elias," and the Arabic version, "Ilyas." The first reference to Elijah merely states that Elijah was counted among the righteous along with Zecharias, John, and Jesus (see Koran 6:86). The second reference recounts the biblical story of Elijah's confrontation with the priests of Baal, telling of Elijah's denouncement of idolatry and his subsequent victory over the wicked priests (see Koran 37:123–30). The translation of a man named "Idris" is mentioned in the text of the Koran, but the name Idris is usually associated with the prophet Enoch. There is no further mention of Elijah in the Koran.

Many of Elijah's characteristics that we saw in the Jewish legends are also found in Islamic legends. In Islamic lore, for example, Elijah has the power of being omnipresent and often shows up at various locations on Friday—the Islamic holy day—to pray at the mosque.[1] Islamic legends sometimes refer to him as the "apostle" that was sent to keep the people from Baal worship.[2] He has the ability to assume many different guises[3] and often comes mounted on a white horse.[4] He reportedly brings rain[5] and is the patron of fertility, particularly for women.[6] Islamic lore also reports that Elijah can save those caught in life-threatening situations, whether they are on land or at sea.[7] He is frequently referred to as the guardian of the desert.[8]

In addition to the Islamic variations of Jewish traditions, there also exist cases in which biblical stories are taken out of their Jewish context and placed in an Islamic setting. For example, there is an Islamic tradition that closely parallels Elijah's confrontation with Ahab. It states that Elijah was sent to preach to the inhabitants of Doele, Syria. The king of the land liked Elijah so much that he made him his vizier. Shortly thereafter, however, the king apostatized and Elijah cursed the entire land of Syria with a famine.[9]

One Islamic tradition that contrasts with Christian and Jewish tradition concerns the fate of the child whom Elijah healed in Zarephath. As previously mentioned in the chapters on Jewish and Christian lore, the boy was believed to be the prophet Jonah. Islamic tradition, however, states that the child was actually Elisha, the future servant and successor of Elijah.[10]

As noted previously in the text, Elijah's translation has been at the center of traditional lore in both the Christian and Jewish spheres—Islamic Elijah lore is no exception. According to the Islamic version of the story, Elijah's translation occurred when Allah commanded him to step outside the house in which he was staying. Upon leaving the house, Elijah spotted a divinely sent horse. Following Allah's command for Elijah to mount the horse, Allah covered him with feathers, enveloped him in fire, and took from him the desire for food and drink so that he could be like the other angels.[11] This translation transformed Elijah into a being that is half-human and half-angel,[12] which enables him to span both earthly and heavenly realms.[13]

Sometimes, as is seen in the Christian correlation of John the Baptist and Elijah, there is a tendency to combine contemporary heroes with prophetic personalities of the past. In Islam, this occurs with Elijah as he is often identified with and claimed to be the same as a legendary figure known as Al-Khadir. In the stories surrounding this Islamic folk hero, he demonstrated many of the same powers and abilities as Elijah. His name literally means "the green man"[14] and most likely stems from his ability to bring rain and make things green. He reportedly found the fountain of youth[15] and, after partaking of the waters of this fountain, became immortal. Because of his immortality and ability to invoke rain, Elijah is often thought to be Al-Khadir. Most scholars, however, believe that they are two distinct individuals that have simply become confused through the ages.[16]

NOTES

PREFACE

1. Boyd K. Packer, *The Holy Temple* (Salt Lake City: Bookcraft, 1980), 98.

Chapter One
THE SETTING

1. William Hamilton Barnes, *Studies in the Chronology of the Divided Monarchy of Israel* (Harvard University, 1991), 153.

2. Harvey E. Filey, "The Book of Kings," in *Beacon Bible Commentary* (Kansas City: Beacon Hill Press, 1969), 338.

3. 1 Kings 9:14; 15:25–26, 33–34; 16:18–19.

4. André Parrot, *Samaria: The Capital of the Kingdom of Israel*, trans. S. H. Hooke, Studies in Biblical Archaeology, no. 7 (New York: Philosophical Library, 1958), 63–72.

5. A. Leo Oppenheim, trans., "Babylonian and Assyrian Historical Texts," in *Ancient Near Eastern Texts Relating to the Old Testament*, ed. James B. Pritchard (Princeton, N.J.: Princeton University Press, 1950), 280–85.

6. H. Jacob Katzenstein, *The History of Tyre* (Jerusalem: Schocken Institute for Jewish Research, 1973), 9.

7. C. F. Keil and F. Delitzsch, *Commentaries on the Old Testament*, vol. 6, trans. James Martin (Grand Rapids, Mich.: Eerdmans, 1949), 228.

8. Katzenstein, *History of Tyre*, 129.

9. Ibid., 144.

10. Alfred Edersheim, *Bible History: Old Testament*, 7 vols. (1876–87; reprint, 7 vols. in 1, Grand Rapids, Mich.: Eerdmans, 1987), 5:178.

11. Oppenheim, "Babylonian and Historical Texts," 278–79.

12. Right Reverend Joseph Hall, D.D., *Contemplations on the Historical Passages of the Old and New Testaments* (London: T. Nelson and Sons, 1882), 279.

Chapter Two
THE CONFRONTATION AND THE BROOK

1. Joseph Longking, "Elijah the Tishbite a Gentile," *Methodist Review* (November 1888): 901–11.
2. George Arthur Buttrick et al., eds., *The Interpreter's Bible*, 12 vols. (Nashville: Abingdon Press, 1952–57), 3:144–45.
3. Adam Clarke, *The Holy Bible, . . . with a Commentary and Critical Notes*, vol. 2 (New York: Phillips and Hunt, 1830), 452.
4. John A. Widtsoe, "Elijah, the Tishbite," *Utah Genealogical and Historical Magazine* 27 (April 1936): 55.
5. Buttrick et al., *Interpreter's Bible*, 3:145.
6. Louis Ginzberg, *The Legends of the Jews*, 7 vols. (Philadelphia: Jewish Publication Society of America, 1909–38), 4:195–96.
7. Clarke, *The Holy Bible*, 454–55.
8. John Gray, *I & II Kings: A Commentary*, 2d ed., rev. (Philadelphia: Westminster Press, 1970), 378.

Chapter Three
THE MIRACLES AT ZAREPHATH

1. Alfred Edersheim, *Bible History: Old Testament*, 7 vols. (1876–87; reprint, 7 vols. in 1, Grand Rapids, Mich.: Eerdmans, 1987), 5:195.

Chapter Four
THE MEETING OF PROPHET AND KING

1. Paul Billerbeck, *Die Briefe Des Neuen Testaments und Di Offenbarung Johannis* (Munich: C. H. Beck'sche Verlagsbuchhandlung, 1954), 760–61.
2. Flavius Josephus, *Antiquities of the Jews*, 8.2.2; see William Whiston, trans., *Josephus: Complete Works* (Grand Rapids, Mich.: Kregel Publications, 1978), 172.
3. James A. Montgomery, *A Critical and Exegetical Commentary on the Book of Kings*, 2d ed. (Edinburgh: T. and T. Clark, 1960), 293.
4. Billerbeck, *Die Briefe*, 760–61.
5. William Lindsay Elexander, ed. (originally edited by John Kitto), *A Cyclopaedia of Biblical Literature*, vol. 1 (Edinburgh: Adam and Charles Black, 1869), 450–51.

Chapter Five
THE CHALLENGE

1. See Thomas S. Monson, "Courage Counts," *Ensign* 16 (November 1986): 40–42.
2. *New American Bible* (Catholic Press, 1970).
3. *The New English Bible* (Oxford and Cambridge University Presses, 1970).
4. *The Jerusalem Bible* (New York: Doubleday, 1968).
5. *The Holy Bible: New International Version* (Grand Rapids, Mich.: Zondervan, 1984).
6. John Gray, *I & II Kings: A Commentary*, 2d ed., rev. (Philadelphia: Westminster Press, 1970), 388.
7. Adam Clarke, *The Holy Bible, . . . with a Commentary and Critical Notes*, vol. 2 (New York: Phillips and Hunt, 1830), 457.
8. Elie Wiesel, *Five Biblical Portraits* (Notre Dame: University of Notre Dame, c. 1981), 45.

Chapter Six
THE PREPARATION

1. Quoted in John Gray, *I & II Kings: A Commentary*, 2d ed., rev. (Philadelphia: Westminster Press, 1970), 402.
2. Joseph Smith, *Teachings of the Prophet Joseph Smith*, sel. Joseph Fielding Smith (Salt Lake City: Deseret Book Co., 1938), 181.
3. Louis Ginzberg, *The Legends of the Jews*, 7 vols. (Philadelphia: Jewish Publication Society of America, 1909–38), 4:198.
4. James A. Montgomery, *A Critical and Exegetical Commentary on the Book of Kings*, 2d ed. (Edinburgh: T. and T. Clark, 1960), 302.
5. Smith, *Teachings*, 277.
6. Ibid., 277–78.
7. Marion G. Romney, in Conference Report, October 1960, 75.
8. Flavius Josephus, *Antiquities of the Jews*, 14.4.3; see William Whiston, trans., *Josephus: Complete Works* (Grand Rapids, Mich.: Kregel Publications, 1978), 292.

Chapter Seven
THE TRIUMPH AT CARMEL

1. Joseph Smith, *Teachings of the Prophet Joseph Smith*, sel. Joseph Fielding Smith (Salt Lake City: Deseret Book Co., 1938), 367.
2. Roger Breuil, *La Puissance d'Elie* (Neuchatel et Paris, Editions Delachaux and Neistle S. A., 1945), 89.

3. Alfred Edersheim, *Bible History: Old Testament*, 7 vols. (1876–87; reprint, 7 vols. in 1, Grand Rapids, Mich.: Eerdmans, 1987), 6:20.

4. Joseph Smith, *The Personal Writings of Joseph Smith*, comp. and ed. Dean C. Jessee (Salt Lake City: Deseret Book Co., 1984), 288; spelling, capitalization, and punctuation standardized.

Chapter Eight
THE REVELATION AT HOREB

1. *Vetus Testamentum*, vol. 25, fasc. 1, 110.

2. Joseph Smith, *Teachings of the Prophet Joseph Smith*, sel. Joseph Fielding Smith (Salt Lake City: Deseret Book Co., 1938), 149–51.

Chapter Nine
THE VINEYARD OF NABOTH

1. Alfred Edersheim, *Bible History: Old Testament*, 7 vols. (1876–87; reprint, 7 vols. in 1, Grand Rapids, Mich.: Eerdmans, 1987), 6:48.

2. *The New English Bible* (Oxford and Cambridge University Presses, 1970).

Chapter Ten
THE DEATHS OF AHAB AND AHAZIAH

1. *The Holy Bible: New International Version* (Grand Rapids, Mich.: Zondervan, 1984).

2. C. F. Keil and F. Delitzsch, *Commentaries on the Old Testament*, vol. 6, trans. James Martin (Grand Rapids, Mich.: Eerdmans, 1949), 287; see also George Arthur Buttrick et al., eds., *The Interpreter's Bible*, 12 vols. (Nashville: Abingdon Press, 1952–57), 3:191.

Chapter Twelve
THE DEPARTURE

1. Joseph Smith, *Teachings of the Prophet Joseph Smith*, sel. Joseph Fielding Smith (Salt Lake City: Deseret Book Co., 1938), 367.

2. Ibid., 325.

Chapter Thirteen
THE DOCTRINE OF TRANSLATION

1. Joseph Smith, *Teachings of the Prophet Joseph Smith*, sel. Joseph Fielding Smith (Salt Lake City: Deseret Book Co., 1938), 171.

2. Ibid., 191.
3. Ibid., 170.

Chapter Fourteen
ELIJAH IN THE NEW TESTAMENT

1. Donald Senior et al., *The Catholic Study Bible* (New York: Oxford University Press, 1990), 872–73.
2. Ephraim E. Urbach, *The Sages: Their Concepts and Beliefs*, trans. Israel Abrahams (Jerusalem: Magnes Press, Hebrew University, 1979), 660–61.
3. Joseph Smith, *Teachings of the Prophet Joseph Smith*, sel. Joseph Fielding Smith (Salt Lake City: Deseret Book Co., 1938), 335–36.
4. Ibid.

Chapter Fifteen
ELIJAH AND THE MOUNT OF TRANSFIGURATION

1. Joseph Fielding Smith, *Doctrines of Salvation*, comp. Bruce R. McConkie, 3 vols. (Salt Lake City: Bookcraft, 1954–56), 2:119.
2. Boyd K. Packer, *The Holy Temple* (Salt Lake City: Bookcraft, 1980), 82.
3. Ibid., 109.
4. Ibid., 84.

Chapter Sixteen
THE PROMISE OF ELIJAH'S RETURN RENEWED

1. "O Little Town of Bethlehem," *Hymns*, no. 208.

Chapter Seventeen
THE DAWNING OF A BRIGHTER DAY

1. "The Morning Breaks," *Hymns*, no. 1.
2. Joshua Sharp, *Astronomical Calendar; or, Farmers' Almanac for 1823* (Ithaca: A. P. Searing and Co., 1823). Located in Cornell University library.
3. As examples, see *Truth Restored: A Short History of The Church of Jesus Christ of Latter-day Saints* (Salt Lake City: The Church of Jesus Christ of Latter-day Saints, 1995); Ivan J. Barrett, *Joseph Smith and the Restoration: A History of the Church to 1846* (Provo, Utah: Brigham Young University Press, 1973); and George Q. Cannon, *Life of Joseph Smith the Prophet*, Classics in Mormon Literature (Salt Lake City: Deseret Book Co., 1986).

4. Joseph Smith, *History of The Church of Jesus Christ of Latter-day Saints*, ed. B. H. Roberts, 2d ed., rev., 7 vols. (Salt Lake City: The Church of Jesus Christ of Latter-day Saints, 1932–51), 1:199.

5. See discourse of Brigham Young, in *Journal of Discourses*, 26 vols. (London: Latter-day Saints' Book Depot, 1854–86), 2:31.

6. Smith, *History of the Church*, 1:400.

7. Ibid., 2:428.

Chapter Eighteen

THE VISITATION OF ELIJAH AT KIRTLAND

1. Stephen D. Ricks, "The Appearance of Elijah and Moses in the Kirtland Temple and the Jewish Passover," *BYU Studies* 23 (Fall 1983): 483–86. See Appendix F herein.

2. Joseph Fielding Smith, *Doctrines of Salvation*, comp. Bruce R. McConkie, 3 vols. (Salt Lake City: Bookcraft, 1954–56), 3:127.

3. Ibid.

4. Bruce R. McConkie, *The Lord God of Joseph Smith*, Brigham Young University Speeches of the Year (Provo, Utah, 4 January 1972), 1.

5. Joseph Smith, *Teachings of the Prophet Joseph Smith*, sel. Joseph Fielding Smith (Salt Lake City: Deseret Book Co., 1938), 172.

6. Joseph Fielding Smith, *Doctrines of Salvation*, 3:129.

7. Boyd K. Packer, "Ordinances," in *1980 Devotional Speeches of the Year: BYU Devotional and Fireside Addresses* (Provo, Utah: Brigham Young University Press, 1981), 16.

8. Joseph Fielding Smith, *Doctrines of Salvation*, 2:165.

Chapter Nineteen

LINE UPON LINE

1. Joseph Smith, *History of The Church of Jesus Christ of Latter-day Saints*, ed. B. H. Roberts, 2d ed., rev., 7 vols. (Salt Lake City: The Church of Jesus Christ of Latter-day Saints, 1932–51), 6:184.

2. Joseph Smith, *The Words of Joseph Smith*, comp. and ed. Andrew F. Ehat and Lyndon W. Cook (Provo, Utah: Grandin Book Co., 1994), 240; spelling, capitalization, and punctuation standardized.

3. Ibid., 335; spelling, capitalization, and punctuation standardized.

4. Joseph Smith, *Teachings of the Prophet Joseph Smith*, sel. Joseph Fielding Smith (Salt Lake City: Deseret Book Co., 1938), 307–8.

5. Quoted in Joseph Smith, *Words*, 49.

6. Robert L. Millet and Joseph Fielding McConkie, *The Life Beyond* (Salt Lake City: Bookcraft, 1986), 90.

7. Joseph Smith, *Teachings*, 179.

8. See discourse of Wilford Woodruff, in *Journal of Discourses*, 26 vols. (London: Latter-day Saints' Book Depot, 1854–86), 5:85.

9. Joseph Smith, *History of the Church*, 4:186.

10. Joseph Smith, *Teachings*, 337.

11. Ibid., 338.

12. Ibid.

13. Joseph Fielding Smith, "Magnifying Our Callings in the Priesthood," *Improvement Era* 73 (June 1970): 65–66.

14. Howard W. Hunter, " 'Exceeding Great and Precious Promises,' " *Ensign* 24 (November 1994): 8.

15. Howard W. Hunter, "The Great Symbol of Our Membership," *Ensign* 24 (October 1994): 5.

Chapter Twenty

THE SPIRIT OF ELIJAH

1. Joseph Fielding Smith, *Doctrines of Salvation*, comp. Bruce R. McConkie, 3 vols. (Salt Lake City: Bookcraft, 1954–56), 3:130.

2. Brigham Young, *Manuscript History of Brigham Young, 1846–1847*, ed. Elden J. Watson (Salt Lake City: Elden J. Watson, 1971), 530.

3. John A. Widtsoe, "Elijah, the Tishbite," *Utah Genealogical and Historical Magazine* 27 (April 1936): 54.

4. Joseph Smith, *History of The Church of Jesus Christ of Latter-day Saints*, ed. B. H. Roberts, 2d ed., rev., 7 vols. (Salt Lake City: The Church of Jesus Christ of Latter-day Saints, 1932–51), 6:184.

5. Ibid., 6:254.

6. Joseph Fielding Smith, *Doctrines of Salvation*, 2:124–25.

7. Ibid., 2:127–28.

8. Ibid., 2:44.

9. Boyd K. Packer, "A Tribute to Women," *Ensign* 19 (July 1989): 74.

Chapter Twenty-One

WHITHER GOEST THOU, ELIJAH?

1. Ezra Taft Benson, "What I Hope You Will Teach Your Children About the Temple," *Ensign* 15 (August 1985): 6–10.

2. Brigham Young, in *Journal of Discourses*, 26 vols. (London: Latter-day Saints' Book Depot, 1854–86), 6:295.

3. Spencer W. Kimball, address at Washington Temple dedication, 19 November 1974, as quoted in Theodore M. Burton, *God's Greatest Gift* (Salt Lake City: Deseret Book Co., 1976), 269. See also Spencer W. Kimball, *The*

Teachings of Spencer W. Kimball, ed. Edward L. Kimball (Salt Lake City: Bookcraft, 1982), 539.

4. Boyd K. Packer, *The Holy Temple* (Salt Lake City: Bookcraft, 1980), 238–39.

5. Joseph F. Smith, in Conference Report, April 1916, 2, 3.

6. Spencer W. Kimball, quoted in Neal A. Maxwell, "Spencer, the Beloved: Leader-Servant," *Ensign* 15 (December 1985): 17, 19.

7. Melvin J. Ballard, *Three Degrees of Glory* [pamphlet] (Ogden, Utah: Neuteboom Ptg., 1929), 30.

8. John A. Widtsoe, "Genealogical Activities in Europe," *Utah Genealogical and Historical Magazine* 22 (July 1931): 104.

9. See discourse of Wilford Woodruff, in *Journal of Discourses*, 19:230.

10. Joseph Smith, *History of The Church of Jesus Christ of Latter-day Saints*, ed. B. H. Roberts, 2d ed., rev., 7 vols. (Salt Lake City: The Church of Jesus Christ of Latter-day Saints, 1932–51), 4:540.

11. Ibid., 3:386–87.

12. John A. Widtsoe, "Temple Worship," *Utah Genealogical and Historical Magazine* 12 (April 1921): 64.

Appendix A

JEWISH TRADITIONS ABOUT THE HISTORICAL ELIJAH

1. Frieda Clark Hyman, "Elijah: Accuser and Defender," *Judaism* 39 (Summer 1990): 288; see also Louis Ginzberg, *The Legends of the Jews*, 7 vols. (Philadelphia: Jewish Publication Society of America, 1909–38), 6:316.

2. Ginzberg, *Legends*, 6:317.

3. Ibid., 5:96; 6:317.

4. Ibid., 6:317.

5. Ibid., 4:196.

6. Ibid., 4:197.

7. Ibid., 6:318.

8. Ibid., 4:197. Tradition also states that the boy could have been the Messiah ben Joseph (ibid., 6:317).

9. *The Jewish Encyclopedia*, 12 vols. (New York: Funk and Wagnalls, 1901–6), 5:122; see also Ginzberg, *Legends*, 4:198.

10. Ginzberg, *Legends*, 4:198.

11. Ibid., 4:199; see also *The Jewish Encyclopedia*, 5:123.

12. Ginzberg, *Legends*, 6:320; 4:199.

13. Ibid., 6:321; 4:199.

14. Ibid., 4:199.

15. Ibid.

16. Ibid., 4:200.

17. Babylonian Talmud (London: Soncino Press, 1935–48), MEGILLAH 19b, p. 119; see also Hyman, "Elijah," 287.

18. Talmud, ABOTH, p. 64; see also Ginzberg, *Legends*, 1:83.

19. *The Jewish Encyclopedia*, 5:123; see also Ginzberg, *Legends*, 4:200.

20. Ginzberg, *Legends*, 6:322.

21. Ibid., 4:239.

Appendix B

JEWISH TRADITIONS ABOUT ELIJAH AS A HEALER AND HELPER

1. Babylonian Talmud (London: Soncino Press, 1935–48), SHAB-BATH 109b, p. 534; see also Louis Ginzberg, *The Legends of the Jews*, 7 vols. (Philadelphia: Jewish Publication Society of America, 1909–38), 4:208, and *The Universal Jewish Encyclopedia* (New York: Universal Jewish Encyclopedia, 1939), 75.

2. John Bowman, "Elijah and the Pauline Jesus Christ," *Abr-Nahraim* 26 (1988): 11; see also Ginzberg, *Legends*, 4:208–9.

3. Ginzberg, *Legends*, 4:205–6.

4. *Encyclopedia Judaica* (Jerusalem: Keter Publishing House Jerusalem Ltd., 1972), 6:638–40.

5. Talmud, BABA KAMMA 60b, p. 350; see also Ginzberg, *Legends*, 6:328, and *The Jewish Encyclopedia*, 12 vols. (New York: Funk and Wagnalls, 1901–6), 5:123.

6. Ginzberg, *Legends*, 6:316.

7. Ibid., 6:334.

8. Ibid.

9. Talmud, TA 'ANITH 21a, p. 105, and SANHEDRIN 109a, p. 747; see also *The Jewish Encyclopedia*, 5:124, and Ginzberg, *Legends*, 6:203.

Appendix C

JEWISH TRADITIONS ABOUT ELIJAH AS A TEACHER AND REVELATOR

1. *The Jewish Encyclopedia*, 12 vols. (New York: Funk and Wagnalls, 1901–6), 5:124.

2. Louis Ginzberg, *The Legends of the Jews*, 7 vols. (Philadelphia: Jewish Publication Society of America, 1909–38), 4:216.

3. Alan Unterman, *Dictionary of Jewish Lore and Legend* (London: Thames and Hudson, 1991), 182. The Shema consists of Deuteronomy 6:4–9, 11:13–21; Numbers 15:37–41.

4. Ginzberg, *Legends*, 6:334–5.

5. Ibid., 6:335.
6. Ginzberg, *Legends*, 4:226; see also *The Jewish Encyclopedia*, 5:125.
7. *The Jewish Encyclopedia*, 5:125; see also Ginzberg, *Legends*, 4:223.
8. Ginzberg, *Legends*, 4:231.
9. *The Jewish Encyclopedia*, 5:126; see also Ginzberg, *Legends*, 6:326.
10. Ginzberg, *Legends*, 4:219–20.

Appendix D

JEWISH TRADITIONS ABOUT ELIJAH IN THE HEAVENLY REALM

1. John Bowman, "Elijah and the Pauline Jesus Christ," *Abr-Nahraim* 26 (1988): 16.
2. Ibid., 5; see also Louis Ginzberg, *The Legends of the Jews*, 7 vols. (Philadelphia: Jewish Publication Society of America, 1909–38), 6:201, *The Jewish Encyclopedia*, 12 vols. (New York: Funk and Wagnalls, 1901–6), 5:123, and Gustav Davidson, *A Dictionary of Angels, Including the Fallen Angels* (New York: Free Press, 1967), 104.
3. Ginzberg, *Legends*, 4:159.
4. Ginzberg, *Legends*, 6:323; 6:37; see also *The Jewish Encyclopedia*, 5:123. It is interesting to note the tradition that Elijah and Moses are not *in* heaven but *near* it and that they are still involved with affairs on the earth. This seems reminiscent of the doctrine taught by Joseph Smith that translated beings exist in a terrestrial state as opposed to a celestial state and that they have been reserved for future missions. See *Teachings of the Prophet Joseph Smith*, sel. Joseph Fielding Smith (Salt Lake City: Deseret Book Co., 1938), 170, 171, 191.
5. Davidson, *Dictionary of Angels*, 257.
6. Ibid.
7. Ibid., 104.
8. Ibid., 257.
9. Bowman, "Elijah," 5.
10. Ginzberg, *Legends*, 6:324; 6:201; see also Davidson, *Dictionary of Angels*, 257, and Bowman, "Elijah," 10.
11. Ginzberg, *Legends*, 6:201; see also *The Jewish Encyclopedia*, 5:123, and Bowman, "Elijah," 5, 10. This sounds much like our doctrine of salvation for the dead, with which Elijah is so inextricably linked.
12. Bowman, "Elijah," 9; see also Ginzberg, *Legends*, 6:446; 5:129.
13. Ginzberg, *Legends*, 6:324.
14. Ibid, 4:389.

Appendix E
JEWISH TRADITIONS ABOUT ELIJAH AS A DEFENDER OF THE COVENANT AND THE FAMILY

1. John Bowman, "Elijah and the Pauline Jesus Christ," *Abr-Nahraim* 26 (1988): 2.
2. *The Universal Jewish Encyclopedia* (New York: Universal Jewish Encyclopedia, 1939), 75, and *The Jewish Encyclopedia*, 12 vols. (New York: Funk and Wagnalls, 1901–6), 5:127.
3. *The Jewish Encyclopedia*, 5:127.
4. Bowman, "Elijah," 2.
5. *The Jewish Encyclopedia*, 5:127; see also Ginzberg, *The Legends of the Jews*, 7 vols. (Philadelphia: Jewish Publication Society of America, 1909–38), 6:338.
6. Ibid.
7. J. Louis Martyn, "We Have Found Elijah," in *Jews, Greeks and Christians: Religious Cultures in Late Antiquity: Essays in Honor of William David Davies*, ed. R. Hamerton-Kelly and R. Scroggs (Leiden: Brill, 1976), 184.
8. Morris M. Faierstein, "Why Do the Scribes Say That Elijah Must Come First?" *Journal of Biblical Literature* 100 (March 1981): 82; see also N. Wieder, "The Doctrine of the Two Messiahs Among the Karaites," *Journal of Jewish Studies* 6 (1955): 16–17.
9. Ginzberg, *Legends*, 6:324.
10. Ibid.
11. *The Universal Jewish Encyclopedia*, 75; see also Ginzberg, *Legends*, 6:338.
12. Ginzberg, *Legends*, 6:339.

Appendix F
JEWISH TRADITIONS ABOUT ELIJAH AND THE PASSOVER

1. Ruth Gruber Fredman, *The Passover Seder: Afikoman in Exile* (Philadelphia: University of Pennsylvania Press, 1981), 14, 62; see also Alfred J. Kolatch, *The Jewish Book of Why* (Middle Village, N.Y.: Johathan David Publishers, 1981), 206.
2. John Bowman, "Elijah and the Pauline Jesus Christ," *Abr-Nahraim* 26 (1988): 2.
3. Fredman, *Passover Seder*, 21.
4. Ibid., 45–46.
5. Ibid., 31, 115–21, 152.

6. Ibid., 21.

7. Ibid., 65.

8. Philip Goodman, *The Passover Anthology* (Philadelphia: Jewish Publication Society of America, 1961), 439.

9. Abraham Isaac Sperling, *Reasons for Jewish Customs and Traditions* (New York: Bloch Publishing Co., 1968), 185; see also Goodman, *Passover Anthology*, 439, and Isaac Levy, *A Guide to Passover* (London: Jewish Chronicle Publications, c. 1958), 51.

10. Sperling, *Reasons*, 196; see also Goodman, *Passover Anthology*, 64, and Levy, *Guide*, 52.

Appendix G

JEWISH LEGENDS ABOUT ELIJAH AS THE FORERUNNER OF THE MESSIAH AND RESTORER

1. Babylonian Talmud (London: Soncino Press, 1935–48), BABA MEZIA 3a, p. 6.

2. Talmud, PESAHIM 34b, p. 156; BABA BATHRA, p. 339.

3. Louis Ginzberg, *The Legends of the Jews*, 7 vols. (Philadelphia: Jewish Publication Society of America, 1909–38), 6:233; see also Morris M. Faierstein, "Why Do the Scribes Say That Elijah Must Come First?" *Journal of Biblical Literature* 100 (March 1981): 82.

4. Ginzberg, *Legends*, 6:339.

5. Talmud, MENAHOTH 63a, p. 371; see also Ginzberg, *Legends*, 6:438.

6. *The Jewish Encyclopedia*, 12 vols. (New York: Funk and Wagnalls 1901–6), 5:126.

7. Faierstein, "Elijah Must Come First," 83.

8. Ginzberg, *Legends*, 6:234; see also *The Jewish Encyclopedia*, 5:127, and John Bowman, "Elijah and the Pauline Jesus Christ," *Abr-Nahraim* 26 (1988): 5.

9. Ginzberg, *Legends*, 4:48.

10. Ginzberg, *Legends*, 6:234; see also *The Jewish Encyclopedia*, 5:127.

11. Ginzberg, *Legends*, 6:235, and *The Jewish Encyclopedia*, 5:127.

12. Ginzberg, *Legends*, 6:235; *The Jewish Encyclopedia*, 5:127; and Bowman, "Elijah," 5.

13. Talmud, SUKKAH 52b, p. 251; see also Ginzberg, *Legends*, 6:235; 5:129, and *The Jewish Encyclopedia*, 5:127.

Appendix H

ELIJAH IN CHRISTIAN TRADITION

1. Michael E. Stone and John Strugnell, *Books of Elijah Parts 1–2* (Missoula, Mont.: Scholars Press, 1979), 94.

2. Tertullian, *Treatises on Marriage and Remarriage to His Wife, and Exhortation to Chastity, Monogamy* (New York: Newman Press, 1951), 87–88.

3. Saint Jerome, *Letters* (New York: Newman Press, 1963), 153.

4. Robert Hayward, "Phinehas—The Same Is Elijah: The Origins of Rabbinic Tradition," *Journal of Jewish Studies* 29 (1978): 23; see also Louis Ginzberg, *Legends of the Jews*, 7 vols. (Philadelphia: Jewish Publication Society of America, 1909–38), 6:317.

5. *Egeria: Diary of a Pilgrimage* (New York: Newman Press, 1970), 174.

6. Thomas W. Mackay, "Early Christian Millenarianist Interpretation of the Two Witnesses in John's Apocalypse 11:3–13," in *By Study and Also by Faith*, vol. 1, ed. John M. Lundquist and Stephen D. Ricks (Salt Lake City: Deseret Book Co., 1990), 302, and *Carmel: Its History, Spirit, and Saints* (New York: P. J. Kennedy and Sons, 1927), 7.

7. *New Catholic Encyclopedia*, 5:382.

8. Peter-Thomas Rohrbach, *Journey to Carith: The Story of the Carmelite Order* (Garden City, N.Y.: Doubleday, 1966), 19.

9. *Carmel: Its History, Spirit, and Saints*, 7; see also Andrew Jotischky, *The Perfection of Solitude: Hermits and Monks in the Crusader States* (University Park, Pa.: Pennsylvania State University Press, c. 1995), 106.

10. Rohrbach, *Journey to Carith*, 18.

11. *Carmel: Its History, Spirit, and Saints*, 5.

12. Jotischky, *Perfection of Solitude*, 108.

13. Ibid., 3.

14. Saint Augustine, *The Literal Meaning of Genesis*, vol. 2 (New York: Newman Press, c. 1982), 76.

15. J. Louis Martyn, "We Have Found Elijah," in *Jews, Greeks and Christians: Religious Cultures in Late Antiquity: Essays in Honor of William David Davies*, ed. R. Hamerton-Kelly and R. Scroggs (Leiden: Brill, 1976), 184; Kent Brower, "Elijah in the Markan Passion Narrative," *Journal for the Study of the New Testament* 18 (June 1983): 87; *The Catholic Encyclopedia*, 5:271–72.

16. Saint Paulinus of Nola, *Letters of St. Paulinus of Nola*, vol. 2 (Westminster, Md.: Newman Press, 1966–67), 101.

17. *The Catholic Encyclopedia*, 5:272.

18. Richard Bauckham, "The Martyrdom of Enoch and Elijah," *Journal of Biblical Literature* 95 (1976): 447.

19. Mackay, "Early Christian Interpretation," 229.

20. Cassiodorus, *Cassiodorus: Explanation of the Psalms* (New York: Paulist Press, c. 1990–c. 1991), 7.

21. Morris M. Faierstein, "Why Do the Scribes Say That Elijah Must Come First?" *Journal of Biblical Literature* 100 (March 1981): 85.

22. *New Catholic Encyclopedia*, 5:382; see also Mackay, "Early Christian Interpretation," 302.

23. Mackay, "Early Christian Interpretation," 294, 302.

24. St. Augustine, *The City of God* (Washington, D.C.: Catholic University of America Press, 1962–64), 757–58.

Appendix I
ISLAMIC LORE ABOUT ELIJAH

1. A. Augustinovic, *"El-Khadr" and the Prophet Elijah* (Jerusalem: Franciscan Printing Press, 1972), 52.

2. *Encyclopedia Judaica* (Jerusalem: Keter Publishing House Jerusalem Ltd., 1972), 6:640.

3. *"El-Khadr" and the Prophet Elijah*, 55.

4. Ibid., 52.

5. Ibid., 57.

6. Ibid., 58.

7. *The Encyclopedia of Islam* (Leiden: Brill, 1960), 3:1156.

8. *The Jewish Encyclopedia*, 12 vols. (New York: Funk and Wagnalls, 1901–6), 5:127, and *"El-Khadr" and the Prophet Elijah*, 61.

9. *The Jewish Encyclopedia*, 5:127.

10. Ibid.

11. *The Jewish Encyclopedia*, 5:127, and *"El-Khadr" and the Prophet Elijah*, 50.

12. *The Encyclopedia of Islam*, 3:1156.

13. *The Jewish Encyclopedia*, 5:127.

14. *The Encyclopedia of Islam*, 4:902.

15. Ibid., 4:904.

16. *The Jewish Encyclopedia*, 5:127.

INDEX